Pilgrimage toward Recovery

DARREN LABRECQUE

Bro-Hun Ministries

WESTBOW
PRESS
A DIVISION OF THOMAS NELSON

Scripture taken from the HOLY BIBLE, NEW INTERNATIONAL VERSION®. Copyright © 1973, 1978, 1984 Biblica. Used by permission of Zondervan. All rights reserved.

WestBow Press books may be ordered through booksellers or by contacting:

WestBow Press
A Division of Thomas Nelson
1663 Liberty Drive
Bloomington, IN 47403
www.westbowpress.com
1-(866) 928-1240

Because of the dynamic nature of the Internet, any web addresses or links contained in this book may have changed since publication and may no longer be valid. The views expressed in this work are solely those of the author and do not necessarily reflect the views of the publisher, and the publisher hereby disclaims any responsibility for them.

Any people depicted in stock imagery provided by Thinkstock are models, and such images are being used for illustrative purposes only.

Certain stock imagery © Thinkstock.

ISBN: 978-1-4497-3495-4 (hc)
ISBN: 978-1-4497-3494-7 (sc)
ISBN: 978-1-4497-3493-0 (e)

Library of Congress Control Number: 2011962996

Printed in the United States of America

WestBow Press rev. date: 12/28/2011

Chapter Content

Dedication

This Book is dedicated to all those who struggle with mental illness to give them a manual to live by. I struggle myself, so I thought since I learned to live with my condition, why not teach others how do the same. Life already has enough challenges of its own and having mental illness can make it seem a little overwhelming. I wrote this book with you in mind to guide you on your own *pilgrimage toward recovery* learning to live with it. 2Co 12:7-10 "And lest I should be exalted above measure through the abundance of the revelations, there was given to me a thorn in the flesh, the messenger of Satan to buffet me, lest I should be exalted above measure. For this thing, I be sought the Lord thrice, that it might depart from me. In addition, he said unto me, my grace is sufficient for thee, for His strength made perfect in my weakness. Most gladly therefore will I rather glory in my infirmities, that the power of Christ may rest upon me. Therefore I take pleasure in infirmities, in reproaches, in necessities, in persecutions, in distresses for Christ's sake: for when I am weak, then am I strong."(NIV, 1999)

Chapter I

Martin Luther Syndrome

Martin Luther syndrome is not an actual diagnosis, but is made up to prove a point about explosive anger we face from time to time. Well, it is like this: I discovered that, while transcribing Scripture into the many languages of the people, Martin Luther would throw things when trying to interpret scripture. Martin was famous for throwing his pen or even tossing a book across the room when something became frustrating. Symptoms of my made up Martin Luther syndrome; include becoming frustrated at objects and things you have no control over, which often stems from overly strict parents. You also may fall into this category if you were called stupid as a child or if you feel frustrated when tasks make too many demands of you.

Every day, my father would pick on me, calling me a retard. From that point on, I developed what I call the *Martin Luther syndrome*, because in my mind, everything had to be perfect. I know I can never do things perfectly, but I certainly try harder than most. Psalm 143:4-8 says, "Therefore is my spirit overwhelmed within me; my heart within me is desolate. I remember the days of old; I meditate on all thy works; I muse on the work of thy hands. I stretch forth my hands unto thee: my soul thirsteth after thee, as a thirsty land. Hear me speedily, O LORD: my spirit faileth hide not thy face from me, lest I be like unto them that go down into the pit. Cause me to hear thy loving-kindness in the morning; for in thee do I trust: cause me to know the way wherein I should walk; for I lift up my soul unto thee." (NIV, 1999) King David goes on to say in Psalm 143:9-10, "Deliver me, O LORD, from mine enemies: I flee unto thee to hide me. Teach me to do thy will; for thou art my God: thy spirit is good; lead me into the land of uprightness." (NIV, 1999) David was another person who got overwhelmed a lot—just read the psalms.

I feel that I should know how do to everything most men do because my father always told us he knew everything, and what he didn't know was nonsense. Growing up, my father made me feel like an idiot if I could not do or did not do something right. I was never coordinated in sports like my older brothers, so my father and brothers would pick on me. My father would always ask me questions that he knew I could not answer just so he could laugh at me when I got the answer wrong. If I dropped something or made any kind of "stupid mistake," my father would yell at me, saying, "Watch what you are doing, you idiot." This gave me a complex of perfectionism that I deal with constantly. Martin Luther syndrome may expect you to seek help to complete certain tasks so you do not become angry when you cannot do them.

We all need to come to grips with this dilemma and to do it we must understand one fact: perfectionism is our own worst enemy. Conflicts become burdensome, especially daily tasks that have become harder due to mental illness. Such instances can become particularly stressful for people like you and me. After all, we all have to learn things differently now and needs become less normal. Our tasks do not have to turn into something unpleasant. One of the best ways to resolve a frustration is not to have it develop into a larger problem, such as Martin Luther syndrome. Such work requires you to do some thinking about situations where you become most frustrated. Chances are you may find one or more things built up throughout these situations. Boldly speaking, frustration occurs when our needs and expectations are not met due to our limitations pushing us further than we think we can handle. At times, for example, you may be required to take a break before you have an explosive outburst. The situation might expect you to relax and be quiet and meditate on Scripture to get your head straight.

Most frustrating situations are avoidable if you can relax while trying to understand your limitations and discover ways that you can work around them. Once you understand such limitation, it might be found that such task that make you too frustrated may become less likely. If you are feeling an unpleasant emotion, such as frustration, anger, or impatience, this is usually a good sign that it is time to take a break and come back to your project later. Sometimes your needs and expectations will only become apparent to you after you have gotten into a project that seems over your head. The best way to calm yourself down is to know what makes you feel this way.

If you find that a project you're working on is causing undesired stress or feelings, you should come back to it later. For example, if you are feeling very frustrated and you think that you may not respond well to the project you are working on, you might try to calm yourself down by thinking of a funny comment. Being indirect or beating on a table are signs that you have Martin Luther syndrome. Some other examples of what this would look like are the occasional urges to throw something out of sheer frustration. You may wonder how to interpret these signs when frustrated motives, feelings, or thoughts are coming on. Look for unpleasant remarks, such as swearing or saying, "I am going to throw my mini laptop across the room." In such cases, it may be a good idea to stop what you are doing, move on to something else, and come back to your project later. You will better understand it later. Of course, you will want to wait until you are calmer and the task seems less frustrating before you finish working on it.

When struggling with the Martin Luther Syndrome, there are four to solve it: (1) Identify the topics you can't work with because they cause emotional problems. You may not be able to finish certain tasks if you do not approach them with a clear focus.

(2) Choose things, such as distractions, that can get your mind off the stressful task so that you can go back to it and think more clearly. What do you dislike about the task expected of you? Answer this and you will discover the appropriate response for any frustrating moment.

(3) Recognize the specific task or situation where you are having a particularly hard time meeting the expectations, because limits are not learned or observed unless you see them with a clear conscience.

(4) Remember, you can control your mind. What seems obvious to you even though it may not have been obvious at that particular time? After all, we are in much clearer understanding with what we know than what we do not know.

Martin Luther syndrome is anger that is an involuntary emotional response to a specific situation. This genially arises from a warped philosophy—a way of viewing the world. Its core stems from a poor outlook that you were taught as a child by a commanding parent, condemning you instead of correcting you in good, positive ways. Therapists generally classify anger as appropriate or inappropriate, depending on how the anger outburst occurred. An appropriate and healthy way to express anger is to let it out gradually. Unhealthy outbursts of anger or suppressing anger makes things worse for you and for the person you take your explosive anger out on.

Ten great tips to manage your anger:

1) Say, "I make myself angry; no one has that control over me."
2) Give it up to God and remember that everything is his.

3) Knowing that everything is God's, you can overlook what made you angry.
4) Recognize that people do not make you angry; they are merely the ones we take it out on.
5) Lower your voice and even laugh at why you are mad.
6) Recognize why you're hurt or the fear that caused anger.
7) Recognize that people's abuse is similar to your own abuse.
8) Ask yourself if feeling anger is helping you solve the problem or making it worse.
9) Avoid letting past issues arise. The past is the past; leave it there.
10) Learn to laugh at yourself a little and then say, "This really does not need to make me upset."

Expressing anger helps release a lot of pent-up frustration, and it is true that an outburst of anger is only momentary. Psychological problems often take control of the body, and some psychologists suggest that expressing anger can cause physical damage. What is the alternative to suppressing or expressing your anger? Do not make yourself angry in the first place! Let your anger out, so it will not cause unneeded physical stress on your body.

This view is hopelessly mistaken. Anger is not a physical entity. Consider an opposite sort of feeling, such as love—a feeling that we often ask to continue. Feelings of love, tenderness, and caring often become coping mechanisms. No one would suppose that by expressing such feelings you were lashing out or losing control. Similarly, self-destructive feelings of anger reaffirm and solidify your angry attitude, making your negative feelings more difficult to dispose of. Refraining from expressing explosive anger may be the first step toward avoiding wrong anger entirely.

Scotty Smith says so eloquently that "some fugitives actually long to get caught, some addicts want desperately to get busted, some Christians, especially 'Christian leaders,' crave to be set free from the disparity between their words and their hearts" (Smith). Anger could create in us the same feeling—to crave to be set free from feeling it. Martin Luther syndrome is a concept of anger that we all face from time to time, but you can learn to use anger in the right ways. How many sources can you identify that make you angry? Due to certain strong anger episodes, pressure, and because of emotional and competitive situations where we find ourselves feeling unable to control our explosive anger, aspects of our anger are decided by how we choose to relate to other. Factors out of control and we are less responsive for areas of our anger, which are controllable if we try to learn the correct responses! Even when showing anger in such ways takes a heavier toll stress in our lives. We must prefer to show rightful anger at things that go wrong. Keep yourselves in an upright position to breathe a little a little clearer opening up the airways. Do not convince yourself that you are rightfully, because you are only destroying the lives your family and relationships with others.

Challenges from our daily lives that cloud our sound judgments, delays a good reaction, leaving rise for bad intention, and lack of fulfillment of increasing Martin Luther disorder. To be honest cannot learn self-control if we do not except what we cannot control. This is something I still struggle with myself, having a LDS (Learning Disabled Syndrome) and ADD (Attention Deficit Disorder), plus being an perfectionist attitude doesn't help the matter any. Sometimes it is OK to let out our anger and other times hold it in. I know my wife always reminds me that to get angry at simple mistakes is not *"kosher"*. I am finding out that being a perfectionist will only make you go crazy with anger and it is not worth the time it takes you fuss over it. The Martin Luther syndrome can be a tedious undertaking and drive you mad. I think I am learning that to stop getting frustrated at I cannot do I should remember what I can do. We all make mistakes this t is simple fact in life. The guide to follow is the truth that what we cannot change it go and what we can change strive to do it better the next time.

According to Rick Warren, "You are not an accident. Your birth was no mistake or mishap, and your life is no fluke of nature. Your parents may not have planned you, but God. He was not at surprised at your birth. In fact God expected it." (Warren) I read this and hit me like "a *ton of bricks*" knowing that God loved us even before we were born. If God love us this much than how can we not believe in ourselves? Simple, it has been grained into ourr heads by self-dout and false preseptions. God is a love and holyisness, so LDS (Learning Disabled Syndrome) and ADD (Attention Deficit Disorder), being a perfectionist attitude does not help when God has our fate in stone. The dynamics of having LDS gives deeper understanding in the things we must be change in order to live in God's nature.

Thinking back on past mistakes it amazes by how many people gave me the solution instead, I had to learn the hard way. Sure, who is going to believe a boy with a learning disability? Maybe there is the sort of a pattern here, but I am going to college online-I am "smart", and most people just have to be kidding me, right? I must admit at that point, there is just no excuse. I should have figured out these situations knowing what made me angry or not. I made one of the biggest mistakes that people with mental illness like do, especially learning disability people who have experienced it. I assumed that I just had to know better. In addition, the truth is, I did not know better. There is nothing like life experience in hard Knox, it beats education every day of the week. The only thing better is an education in hard Knox or a willingness to learn from other people's experience.

Mishap, are something we all have from time to time. There are basic learning techniques that any mental illness sufferer knows to live effectively. They do not need to look for something more in life to get involved in, because you know from the experience, as well as the experience of others. You may hear things that seem too simple to be true but listen, you might be amazed. First the theory, and then the practice is we all make mistakes and the golden rule teaches that we can learn from them. Everything makes sense the only opportunity for learning is trying something new. Before there can be learning, there must be learners. It is true wherever there is a written work, no matter how clever or stupid the writer might seem. Whatever the question or problem is discussed, if you do not already know the answer cause someone else figured it out already before you peeked, because God told you! The only way to come up with the answer is to take some creative leaps in the dark and informed by your results. You, who know a little, may actually know the answer to the question at hand. You can take leaps somewhat guided from the outset of your anger by what you already know. Guessing at random never really accomplishes anything.

A fluke of anger is a momentary lapse of reason where we react rather than think about that the situation that is making us angry. We all have those times when we wish that we could take a mistake or unpleasant word back. It is in these times that we discover our true path to recover from Martin Luther Syndrome. As anger rears, its ugly we need to not let it make us feel the need to explode and are anger in a un-impropriate manor. People like us with Martin Luther Syndrome it is like taking a road trip. This would be a road trip to a better you, someone you might actually be proud to know!

According to Pastor Phil Lewis of Park Place, Wesleyan Church in Pinellas Park Florida says it this way; "Drunks do funny things (Romans 8:5), Drunks are out of control (Romans 8:6-9), Drunks are killers (Romans 8:12-13), Drunks are children Romans 8:14-17. Romans 8:5 "For they that are after the flesh do mind the things of the flesh, but they that are after the Spirit do the things of the Spirit." Hear the world would look at this a funny, because it seems irregular to choose not to show emotion. The world says to shout let it all out and to God that seems funny! A prudent man would show his frustration when it does not affect those around him. (Romans 8:6-9) "For to be carnally minded *is* death; but to be spiritually minded *is* life and peace. Because the carnal mind *is* enmity against God for it is not subject to the law of God, neither indeed can be. So, then they that are in the flesh cannot please God, but ye are not in the flesh, but in the Spirit, if so be that the Spirit of God dwell in you. Now if any men have not the Spirit of Christ, he is none of his." We are nothing without Christ the spirit of anger and frustration as no place in us, because we live not by the flesh, but by the Spirit of our Lord Jesus Christ. Pray to him and we will have the strength to overcome our feelings of frustration. (Romans 8:14-17) "For as many as are led by the Spirit of God, they are the sons of God. For ye have not received the spirit of bondage again to fear; but ye have received the Spirit of adoption, whereby we cry, Abba, Father. The Spirit itself beareth witness with our spirit, that we are the children of God: And if children, then heirs; heirs of God, and joint-heirs with Christ; if so be that we suffer with him, that we may be also glorified together." (Lewis, 2010)

If we think about it this way then we have no need to get frustrated! My friend that is a concept I am still trying to learn as I am writing this book. All I can give you for advice is pray—without ceasing. Jesus showed the perfect example of dealing with frustration. Martin Luther Syndrome is a mental illness that is curable by learning to calm the situation. Do not feel you have no hope, there is always hope Life is a series challenges and if we understand this it will be easier to cope with those frustrated times. Heartstrings play what we put into our brain so be true and listen you will discover more about yourself than ever new. Many theories and practices have been made, none our more suitable than relaxing in God's Word. Nothing makes sense when opportunity for learning never met and understood. Before this, we must be learner patterns of breathing and relaxing. Whatever the problem you face be ready find the answer, because will make you regret it! One way to come up with a solution is making giant leaps into the unknown, informed you of the progress. Actually, the answer to the question is to ask a question!

Help me dear Lord to encompass the mind. To come to you in every circumstance I face. Give me the much-needed grace to guide me through my trials. I ask you dear God that in encompassing the mind, help me to escape myself made prison. My Lord, My God, I am one in the open naked and vulnerable, be my strength in my in my struggles. Renew my mind, body, and spirit and give me the necessary tools to reach others who struggle in the same way. Heal me from the Martin Luther Syndrome Amen!

Chapter II

The Hammer of Negativity

The hammer of negativity represents the hurtful things our parents or peers have said in the past that affected us. No one is immune to words they can hurt as well as encourage. My father said he wish he never had a retard for a son and this can be a negative thought that stays with you. Taking positively you can strive to do better and prove people who put you down wrong. Our intellectual part is aware of how negativity is around us affects and drains our spirit. Often times, we are negative with our own self, because of past emotional abuse. This makes us beat ourselves up constantly until we get sick. Live well is the cure, because those who put you down will see the consequence and be tormented of how treated you in the past. Stop being mad at yourself, stop blaming yourself, stop beating yourself up, and it changed your life for the better! When was the last time you look at yourself in a mirror? What did you see as you allow your gazed in the mirror your entire body? What do you see when you look at your eyes, the windows to your soul? Did you like what you saw? To change you, you have to with courage listen to those voices telling you it is OK. The familiar voice is God making you feel worthy, lovable beautiful. God is that joyful voice that says I love you and I recognize you are not perfect and yet I love you anyway.

Life is a learning process, compared to a game of Baseball. In Baseball, a man called a pitcher throws a hardball over a white plate while a catcher catches the ball. Our negative parents are the pitcher and the Devil is the catcher. The batter who hits the baseball with a wooden bat is representative of us. The basemen known as the first basemen, second basemen, third basemen are foes that have it in for us. Right fielder, Center fielder, and Left fielder are the bad teachers in our life. As the pitcher (your negative parents) throw the ball and caught by the catcher (the Devil) we try to hit the ball. Get on first we have found the source to our problems. Get to Second we have found the means to a solution. Get to third we have prayed to Christ Jesus for help. Hit a homerun and you have accepted Christ Jesus into our heart. I believe you can stop putting yourself down and feeling tired, feeling unlovable and unworthy. Come on, stop being mad at yourself and with the rest of the world. You are all you have besides Christ Jesus, so forget your problems for grace is a gift use it and decide to make yourself the most vibrant, wonderful, tender, loving person in the world. I promise you your life will change for the better and you will learn the coping mechanisms to survive. Grace comes from the Greek word gratos—meaning to miss the mark (the red center circle in Archery).

The day I graduated High School I overheard my parents talking and my father said I never wish I had a *"retard"* for a son. It was just a small conversation, but I still remember that incident. I remember this feeling of dread of every time I would do something new. Remembering how frustrated I am doing anything especially if I cannot do the particular task right. I am always afraid of making a mistake, always condemning myself and this fear escalated into what Psychologist refer to as "if I can't do it right, my parents or peers will not love me" saying. Ask yourself is it a crazy thing or not? Three things can stop you from succeeding in life our fear of failure, fear of not being good enough, fear of making mistakes. We all make mistakes so it is okay to fail, because when fail what we learn from it makes us a better person. Do you know the greatest failures become our greatest blessings? Do not fear anymore what you might fail at, do what you love and learn to soar like eagles. **Isaiah 40:31** "But they that wait upon the LORD shall renew their strength; they shall mount up with wings as eagles; they shall run, and not be weary; and they shall walk, and not faint."

Forgiving yourself is the key to dealing with the negative past. The only way to stop getting so mad at yourself is to start forgiving yourself for what obviously is not your fault. Forgive those stupid mistakes we all make them! Forgiveness is a choice we all have to make of those who hurt us, who we have hurt. Let go, allow, and allow God's grace to forgive us to heal the wounds. Get rid of those negativity hammer words. Decide to use positive words you can use in conversations, when you talk. Think about yourself and others as you talk about the in the world around you. Celebrate your little successes as triumphs! Pamper yourself with words of encouragement! Even say to yourself, that you are of proud of you! For instance, being proud of how you handled a situation so calmly. Using negative words impacts how you feel and how your behavior will be. Friends will begin to talk about how depressed you felt, actually contributing to a result getting worse acting on bad choices. Notice the sequence—words that you create having an impact on feelings influencing behavior. It is almost impossible to act positively when using negative words. Note that when you are depressed you use describing moments of prolonged feelings of sadness and hopelessness can be a serious condition that needs the attention of a mental health professional.

Your words affect your present experience, so limiting using words, you will react in a corresponding manner of depression, because we always act the way we describe ourselves. Look at yourself in the mirror and affirming, patting yourself on the shoulder and saying "good job" when your overcome with some difficulty take some time out to celebrate yourself not getting mad! Loving yourself means taking care of you so be the kind to yourself. Nourish your body, your mind, and your spirit with the Holy Scriptures on how wonderful loving person in the whole world you are to God. This is what you are going to give to all those that you meet in this lifetime, you are a beautiful gift from God. Psalm 139:14 "I will praise thee; for I am fearfully *and* wonderfully made: marvelous *are* thy works; and *that* my soul knoweth right well." (NIV, 1999) Negativity does not get us anywhere, but feeling depressed about "old bad news" get my drift! Come on be a person with purpose and show those who put you down what makes you who you are.

The key to be a successful *pilgrim in recovery* is to understand that the hardships we face in life are there to make us a whole and unique person. These become the tools in life to motivate us. "Most of all they give me glamour of God's first love, often at moment when I start feeling depressed and discouraged. You know what the third temptation of Jesus was "*power*" (Nouwen) You do a crazy thing this putting one-self down! For many people it all they know. Fear of failure come from the fear of not being good enough, so it is time to hear this truth. It is okay to make mistakes. We all fall down, but strong person gets up again. There is no shame in failing sometimes that how we learn in life. Do you know our greatest failures often become our greatest accomplishments? No needs to fear when we can fly like eagles do soaring into the eye of the storms. We need to take the initiative. "If used genuinely, initiative implies both a risk and willingness act unilaterally. Our initiatives never involve either. We simply say we will get rid of this if you get rid of that." (Peck, 1987) Initiative is to key to getting whole without it you will always be stuck at stalemate.

Be a motivational and high content person take the initiative and influence those around you to enjoy being around you! However, using humor can be a very challenging at time, because I always described myself as serious, t funny. My readers you need motivational and inspirational skills in your life. I never thought much about being funny, but I finally decided to try humor and it seemed to have a calming effect on others and me around me. I decided to be open to being more humorous instated of throwing a negative pity-party-fit and it had a good result over time I was easily incorporated humorous content into my moments of negativity. People began to see the change a in my motivational style as rather calming. Amazingly, a number of friends told me that I missed my calling and should have been a stand-up comic instead of a off a Peer Mentor and or advocator for people who struggle with Mental Illness. What you might say, did I suddenly discover I had a funny bone? No! By stopping my negative words, I became more able to let my humorous side emerge lessoning the chance of being depressed and negative about myself. I still have the moments when I put myself down, but learned the keys to make them less. Forgive yourself and stop hating yourself! Forgive your mistakes and the choices you might have made. Forgive those situations where mistakes happen and allow God's grace of forgiveness to heal the harm you might have caused. Get rid of those negative words. Negative words only bring you nothing, but thoughts failure and pity. Depression is a miserable place to be, you must decide to be positive and use creative thinking strategies, when you start to think about yourself and others as you deal with the world around you.

Learn something new every time you do a new task, because in everything there is a lesson to learn. Stop saying, "I can't do this, and I can't do that". Just say, "I can do it." Saying yes to going to college is something new for me. I know there are moments when I think I am not good enough and that thought alone can stop me from continuing on, but by saying "I can do it and be able to follow through with goal, which is to finish college getting a degree as a Pastoral Psychologist. Celebrate your triumphs and little successes telling yourself in words how proud of you are, state clearly what you have done. For instance, I am proud of you for handling my mistakes calmly. I sometimes hear my wife saying "good job" when I overcome some difficulty. That helps me a lot! It is OK if you give yourself a treat to celebrate. Loving yourself means taking care of you! Be kind to yourself, be gentle, be tender, and nourish your body, your mind, and your spirit. This is what you are going to give to all those that you meet for a lifetime. You are a beautiful gift from God, the sooner we realize that the better we will be. We are a gift which God the Creator and Father entrusted with inestimable value. From the moment of conception God respected our being in an absolute way, because man is the only creature on earth that God has "wished for himself" and the spiritual soul of each man created by God in the image of the Creator. Believe it when I say life has something greater, the very gift of God's love, which to preserve and make fruitful. "Being included in Gods family is the highest honor and greatest privilege you will ever receive." (Warren R., 2002)

An orderly way of doing things is definitely an important part of organization, simply because were told in the past negative input. This is especially true when we are facing emotionally overwrought, suffering from illness or depression, or experiencing a spiritual crisis. Clearing out this negative energy in our mind is a very simple process and believe me the difference in how your mind feels once you have done it is astounding! All you need are a few simple tools and about an hour of your time. Before you do any kind of energy clearing, you really should get your mind in order as much as possible. An energy clearing your mind will only do so much, but you still got piles of junk in your memory you need get rid. Think of your brain like a computer and negative debris like spyware kept file away. Too much negative debris and the computer (your mind) slow down or crash. Attention is needs to be work on in areas where clutter has been building up for some time. This step may take a little in fact; it may take you more than a day! However, it is a crucial part of the process, so take as long as you do it properly. The effectiveness of your energy clearing will depend on you.1Corinthians 2:5 "That your faith should not stand in the wisdom of men, but in the power of God". (NIV, 1999)1Corinthians 1:5 "That in everything ye are enriched by him, in all utterance, and *in* all knowledge" (NIV, 1999)

Negative thoughts are the enemy of most people in life. Negative thoughts will distract your focus from the important positive ones. At the end, you will no longer have the ingredients necessary for success. Knowing this will help overcome negative thoughts that make the difference between victory and defeat. (1) Realize you only hurt yourself with negative thoughts. (2) Do not let the negative thoughts trick you. (3) Decide that you will change every day happy and content without negative thoughts stealing your joy. (4) Look at yourself in the mirror and saying, I am a positive person I will not let negative thoughts control me. (5) Read positive scripture the Bible at random and interject positive words in your thinking. (6) Change the tone of your thoughts from negative to positive. (7) Remember to stop thinking negative things about shifting your attention to positive things. (8) Smile, because it take more muscles think negatively and frown, than to smiling and think positively. (9) Think and act confidently keeping good body language and positive thoughts. (10) Pray and meditate on God's Word for peace and calmness to overcome negative thoughts.

When it comes to psychology and (the study of the mind), we all discover what I refer to as the Bitterness Plant. This plant starts from a small seed and grows to become an overwhelming presence in our lives. The Bitterness Plant begins when as a child told something so negative that it ingrains itself in the mind and spirit of a child. As the child grows up the negative remarks of the parents and or peers fuels the bitterness. Making the once child now adult physical, mentally, and spiritually sick. This is what Psychiatrist call depression due to chronic abuse. This is where the core issues are that we have tried to hide from the world. My wife Noel always says medication is a band—aid, but God is the antibiotic. I once read of an ancient Chinese Philosopher Lao Zu say; "To journey a million miles one must take the first step." In our case a million miles symbolizes our pilgrimage of life. To overcome the bitterness in our lives, we must take the first step. The first step would be coming to grips with our negative precepts by ways to prove them wrong. By doing this we learn how to turn the negative into positive. We must train our mind as well as our spirit.

This is a concept I am still learning, but here is what I have learned so far: (1) In everything negative there is always something positive. (2) We learn more about ellowourselves while in our depression. (3) Anger is not always a bad thing. (4) Humility is a verture that so few have. (5) Trials are not trials at all, but repercussions from bad choices. (6) Repercussions are not a means of punishment, but the means to teach us. Therefore to recover we must learn and accept a series of six disciplines for true wellness and growth. This my fellow pilgrims rings so true in learning more about ourselves, while in a state of depression. For it is when we are weak that God makes us strong. 2Corinthians 13:9 "Therefore we are glad, when we are weak, and ye are strong: and this also we wish even, perfection." (NIV, 1999) We only need to ask, God what is His true purpose and He will show it through us. How does this happen? I have a learning disability and God's help I constantly defy the odds.

When I say anger is not always a bad thing, I am referring to the difference between appropriate and inappropriate anger. It is not good to explode in an irrational manor, but in respect use your tone to show those around you your disappointment. Jesus shows several examples in the Bible. These examples will show that Jesus showed anger based upon principle. It is all right to stick up for yourself even raise your voice, but how you go about it is something different. God said keep the right attitude and He will, take the wrong attitude away. Mat 21:12 "And Jesus went into the temple of God, and cast out all them that sold and bought in the temple, and overthrew the tables of the moneychangers, and the seats of them that sold doves." (NIV, 1999) Mat 21:13 "Jesus, said unto them it is written, my house, shall be called the house of prayer; but ye have made it a den of thieves." Mat 21:14 (NIV, 1999) Blind and the lame came to him in the temple; and he healed them. Mat 21:15 (NIV, 1999)When the chief priests and scribes saw the wonderful things that he did, and the children crying in the temple, and saying, Hosanna to the Son of David; they were sore displeased, Mat 21:16 And said unto him, Hearest thou what these say? Jesus saith unto them, Yea; have ye never read, Out of the mouth of babes and suckling's thou hast perfected praise?" (NIV, 1999) Here Jesus show anger toward the Pharisees and Scribes, but compassion toward those who came for healing. With a tone of authority, but without yelling he cast all the moneychangers and merchants out who were defiling the temple. Jesus showed here a righteous anger! Keep the right attitude and God will take it all the way home. God can take all our pieces from the hurts of the past, the tortured nightmares from years of abuse, the broken down spirit filled self-doubt; God will take it all and add it up giving us back what we don't deserve. God is the author and finisher of our lives and if we trust Him, He will give us back double for our heartache.

Such a tool as this would be that of *humanity*. Humility is one of the hardest tools God gives us to use, because of our mental instability. We feel the world owes us, but in all aspects the world and God owes us nothing. God gives us what we need and that is grace. Humility may be hard to act upon, but the Bible says that it is the beginning of all wisdom. "Who is wise in understanding among you? Let him show it by his good life, by deeds done with humility that comes from wisdom." (NIV, 1999) (James 3:13) Trials in life come to teach us for if we did not have trials we would know grace. We need to be refined in order to get a perspective on our recovery. "Consider it pure joy, any brothers when you face trials of many kinds, because the testing of your faith develops perseverance. Perseverance must finish its work so that you may mature, not lacking in anything" James 2:1-4 (Meyers). Trials come into our very beings; we can discover wisdom that will help us in our *pilgrimage toward recovery*. By doing this we become examples for others like us to follow. Prayer is a very important part in the recovery process. It is prayer that will give us the strength to lift us out of our circumstance. "Is anyone of you in trouble? He should pray" James5:13 (NIV, 1999). In all aspects of recovery, a person who prays finds true emotional health and growth. Pray about your problem and work out the answer!

Working out the answer comes in many shapes and forms. You can work out your problem by helping someone else or by simply listening to a song. Reading a good book sometimes helps. Calling a friend or family member can also be a way to work out a problem. This step is hard, because it means coming to grips with part of us we hid away for so long. One thing I can say is life is fall of challenges and the *bitterness plant* grows to become as discussed earlier by the six concepts. Taking the six concepts a little further would be getting into the *nitty gritty* of our personal struggle. Life is what we make of it, so if we want it to be better than we need to go to the source. In going to the source, we become one with the one who created us. We our beautifully, and wonderfully made in image of God! Knowing this helps me when I am feeling depressed it uplifts my spirit.

I remember in a book I read by Og Modino called Twelfth Angel about a little boy with cancer who the main character of the book meets when coaching Baseball. The little boy would struggle catching and hitting, but he kept trying and would always say never give up, never give up, you can do it if you try. When dealing with the state of depression we have the tendency to want to "throw in the towel" as they say. Has the boy in OG's story we must never give up! If we try with a little help from God, we can move mountains. When in our tattered state of mind do not be stubborn, ask for help from a caring friend or even God. For some of us it is hard reach out when we have only known abuse and neglect. Believe me there is always a caring person if you look hard enough.

Your Bitterness Plant should become the fuel on your fire to succeed. After you rip out the seed you need to branch out to succeed higher and better than ever imagined, because the world would have nothing to say accept WOW. Let get real, for me writing a book and going to college to become a Pastoral Councilor is nothing short of amazing. I will succeed and has I do you the reader of this book will succeed as well. Doing this by the grace of God working in me it is confirmed, when another person sees me rise above my struggles. I still struggle but God shines through in my weakness. Bitterness does not have to take over and run your live! We need to get rid of it and learn ways to better ourselves. By no means will I ever ask you to stop taking the medication your Psychiatrrist perscribe you, but to *continue taking it*. This book is only to teach you ways to control what the medication doesn't, and that is our subconcious and emotional being. My aim is to give you guidance on how to overcome and learn from the pain we face. This is a *pilgrimage toward recovery* and one that is never going to end, but with proper tools and can become livable and practical for the comfort of you the one who suffers.Remember I said bitterness runs deep, bitterness that effects the brain. It begins to effect the spirit as well, causing us to be sick in the body.

Dear Lord I have I have let the Bitterness Plant grow for too long in my life. Show me how to reach into the depth of my soul and pull out the seed stuck in the soil of my inner man. I came from abused and now I find myself abusing those around me including myself. My thoughts from the past consume my mind, Lord please give a *spiritual bath to wash away my pain and give me grace*, I need to overcome this pain. Help me dear Lord to rebuke the Adversary from reminding of what I have put behind me. Lord please take this broken heart and create in me a new and improved heart!

Chapter III

The Key Too Wholeness

The one question people ask in Psychiatry, is what the key to wholeness? Psychiatrist and individuals have been trying to answer this sense the dawn of time. Your enemy's (Satan) main targeted priority is the arena of your mind. Satan knows that if can control and manipulate your way of thinking he can control your entire life. Most thoughts determine our actions, attitudes, and self-image. In, reality thoughts determine your destiny! That is why the Bible warns us to guard our minds. As Jesus Christ so eloquently pointed out to me in life wholeness is found when seeking eternal things and keeping our guard against the Devil. When we this spiritual truth we begin to develop a pattern of wholeness and in return find our destiny {*pilgrimage toward recovery*}

We will stumble from time to time, but in true discovery, we find the answer. Instead of wondering why we are in a certain circumstance, we should be asking, what is Jesus trying to teach me? Everything is a learning experience and or a challenge to face head on. If we begin to see our emotional problems this way they become easier to deal with. Our emotional condition is not a bad thing! In fact, in some aspects it is a blessing. I believe it can be a blessing, because if we learn to accept it we gain *God given wisdom*. To be whole we must know the author of wisdom. "Trust in the Lord with all heart and lean not in your own understanding; in all your ways acknowledge Him, and He will make your paths straight" Proverbs 3:5-6 (NIV, 1999).

Depression and anxiety can cause physical symptoms as well. Have you ever heard how someone died of a "broken heart"? Well it is true! Depression runs deep, effecting the mind, body, and soul. Leading Psychologists document that depression and stress causes the most heart attacks. "Do not be wise in your own eyes, but fear the Lord and shun evil. This will bring health to your body and nourishment to your bones" Proverbs 3:7-8 (NIV, 1999). To receive victory over depression we must lean on God instead of our own self. *"The heart finds peace in the Loving arms of God."* People like you and I have a time dialing with stress. In fact, dealing with it takes some effort on our part. *Sometimes we need to be still to hear the voice of the Lord.* Be silent before God and He will guide you every step of the way.

To grasp wholeness we must grasp grace! Grace is a God given gift to us by God to empower us in our *pilgrimage toward recovery*. There are two sides to grace and they are suffering and joyfulness. In suffering, you learn the purpose for needing grace. If we do not endure suffering, we would not be able to grasp grace. Christ had to suffer even on to death on a cross for us! In like aspect, we must suffer to receive the full knowledge grace. When we experience joy in our lives it comes from suffering and by suffering finding favor with God. The world may see you and me as unwanted, un-needed, but God sees us as perfect.

God does not want clones instead He wants variety and we should not let anyone to shape us other than the image God wants us to be. Do not let the world pressure you into feeling badly about ourselves, because we do not fit their image of who we should be! Some people spend most of the pitiful existence trying to be entirely someone their not. *How ironic!* God does not create junk, so to say we are worthless is to say that God made a mistake. Why would God allow us to have mental instabilities? It simply lies in the fact that in us and through us God can show His strength in our weakness. Take your eyes of your mental illness and put them on Christ Jesus. Put a smile on your face knowing Jesus is by your side. When we fall, He lifts us up and straightens our path so that we can walk in truth.

Ask Jesus my *fellow pilgrim* to allow His strength can show through your weakness for examples for others to follow. Being weak and depressed, but showing merit not only do you show strength, but become lighthouse to those who are lost in the storms of {mental illness}. Asking Jesus what he is doing in our life! You can find the answer in the fact, that your weakness is really the fuel that causes you to change. It takes a conscious effort on our part to break free from depression. I am from time to time still dealing with depression and on a state of recovery, but I have discovered the way to cope. People ask me why I seem to have things under control and keep a good outlook on life. It is simply Jesus Christ working through me and in me! He is my lighthouse! My eyes, has been opened up to a new way of living! You will find out that your life will be in a constant state of recovery. We must step out in faith and challenge ourselves to want to change. One thing I see in my peers and from time to time in me is poor self-image. We our image on what we see and hear in the world of media, do not get worked up about it. No one can really measure up to what the media portrays as "norm". Life is full of disappointments and people will always let down. Why live for a world that will kick you when you are down. There are *"bigger and better things"* to live for and model our life after. Do not be a person who makes excuses, but be a *"person of purpose"* Become a person whom people feel it is an honor to be associated with as a person. We pilgrims in a *pilgrimage toward recovery* and the pilgrimage calls on us to be better than people expect us to be! Recover or an uphill battle, but trust me when I say you will be better for it. You find courage when we step out beyond ourselves and exceed where others say that we cannot.

I am in my own way stepping out in faith, by writing this book and day lecturing on the subject of *mental illness*. I truly believe God will help and guide me on my *pilgrimage toward recover*. Many things I have learned along the way and I have come to know that life can seem like a series test, but when we let them teach us, we gain the life skills to succeed. God delights in seeing us succeed! Why listen to a message and or thought that are when the wisdom that comes from God is true? The Bible says we need not live as one who serves sin, but as one who is set freed from sin. The old man is our past life that we put aside instead of dealing with it and the new man is what we become when we accept Jesus Christ into our spirit being. I used the allegory of taking bath because it is the easiest way to explain what Jesus Christ can do if we let him. If we understand this difference of the contrast between old man, and new man we have learned to encompass the mind. What am I trying to say here? The statement on cues is one of a social and personal response. What cues could we give to someone who is mentally ill? The answer lies in one's ability to change. If I want you to want recovery, I must show you a proven formula that could show you the cue you need to believe in recovery. In the Greek, the word for recovery is anastasis: rise from the dead that should rise, rising again. When we talk about recovery, it is like a raising the dead, because we our dead to the truth and the mind and our subconscious.

To understand, we must first discuss the purpose of life itself. What is the purpose of life? This question been debated and asked by philosophized for centuries. Philosophers from Socrates, to the most resent philosophers of modern day. Greek philosophers were the first who created models to answer this question. Plato and Aristotle came close to answering the question of the purpose of life, but in my opinion, Augustine found the true purpose of life. Plato talks about the forms of true good creating a theistic type of god and his god becomes an unknowing god. Plato lacks to give an adequate and to how human beings obtain the knowledge of God. Plato theory of the god who lives in the forms does not give a true definition of the purpose of life. Aristotle tried to take Plato's forms and make light of them, but in my opinion fell far short of finding a meaningful purpose to life. Both Plato and Aristotle tried intellectually to explain the mind of God. Plato God is one of complex forms that have no rational form in of themselves. I have lived a foolish life and walked in the lust and now I can say that am suffering much harm because of my foolish ways. Know that I found Jesus Christ and walk with those who know him I am growing wiser every day. It is amazing how one verse could have such a profound impact on a person's life. The ultimate purpose in life is this, live for God, and put all other things aside and good things will follow. Pray earnestly and you God will give you over and abundantly. You must understand and follow *The Lord's Prayer,* make this a model for your life and you cannot go wrong.

The Lord's Prayer is the model prayer the Christ Jesus gave his disciples when they asked him how to pray. It must be our model prayer as believers as well and our daily prayers. Modeling this prayer is the best way I know to prayer. This is how my wife and I pray for everything. {1} "Thy kingdom come Thy will be done in earth, as it is in heaven: Means to worship the Lord God. It also calls us to offer up praise of thanksgiving and lift the God up on high. This could entail thanking him for the day or putting on the Amor of God. We can worship him in song and in Spirit. We praise the Lord because as believers we know that He deserves our prayers. We lift him up here on earth and we will have riches stored up in Heaven. I find that outside in nature I can find many things to praise God for, for He is the Creator of everything. His Kingdom is everlasting the Earth is not! {2} "Give us this day our daily bread: Whatever we ask for in Heaven God will do on earth. Mat 6:33 "But, seek ye first the kingdom of God, and his righteousness; and all these things shall be added unto you." (NIV, 1999) Jesus provides our needs so I prayer for my daily needs. My wife and I pray that God provides our needs for the day and bring people into our live that we can bless or can be a blessing to us.

Daily Bread comes in many forms like a kind word, or money needed, a scripture verse, or an affirmation, extra. {3} "And forgive us our debts, as we forgive our debtors: This is to some the hardest to do, because hurt runs deep. Although when you forgive someone, it releases a load off your shoulders and your heart. Forgiving is the one we as believers all dread. My wife and I make this are daily prayer as we go to bed at night and as we wake up in the morning. Systematically day by day asking for forgiveness lightens the load of burdens bared. {4} "And lead us not into temptation, but deliver us from evil: The devil throws temptation at us in every way and in every form. He is the Master of Lies and the Deceiver of the Brethren. My wife and every morning prayer to put on the Armor of God mentioned in: Eph 6:11-17 "Put on the whole armor of God, that ye may be able to stand against the wiles of the devil against principalities, against powers, against the rulers of the darkness of this world, against spiritual wickedness in high places. Wherefore, take unto you the whole armor of God that ye may be able to withstand in the evil day, and having done all, to stand. Stand therefore, having your loins girt about with truth, and having on the breastplate of righteousness; And your feet shod with the preparation of the gospel of peace; Above all, taking the shield of faith, wherewith ye shall be able to quench all the fiery darts of the wicked. And take the helmet of salvation, and the sword of the Spirit, which is the word of God." {5} "For thine is the kingdom, and the power, and the glory, forever. Amen." We end our prayer with giving praise and thanks for what God has done and will do in our lives. Giving Him rule in our lives and all power and glory for every avenue of our lives. He is the Author and finisher of His creation, so why not give all to him. Jesus taught us this way and Christ Jesus is God in the flesh, so whatever the Son of God says we must do likewise.

Again, I must repeat the key to wholeness in terms is Psychological funk that we as individuals get into from time to time. This stems from the word vulnerability usually cause by some emotional hurt. "The word "vulnerability" is also ambiguous because it does not distinguish between physical and emotional wounding. It is not just that as children, we will not be able to climb trees without risking scraped knees; it is more a matter of emotional pain. There is no way we can live a rich life unless we are willing to suffer repeatedly, experiencing depression and despair, fear and anxiety, grief and sadness, anger and the agony of forgiveness, confusion and doubt, criticism and it rejection. A life lacking these emotional upheavals will not only be useless to ourselves, will be useless to others. We cannot be healed without being willing to be hurt." (Dr. M. Scott Peck, 1987) It is in understanding the emotional upheavals that we grow and begin to recover. Depression and Anxiety begin when we refuse to deal with the past hurts. If we are not willing to be hurt then we become useless in our own eyes. I want to teach you to avoid pinnacle point of mental illness.

The ability to stand up to grow to inspire to criticism is to have discovered the beginning of the *pilgrimage toward recovery* being well on the way to success. Criticism as two forms one being negative annotation and the other being positive annotation, each one being crucial to us as *pilgrims toward recovery.* You can criticize someone positively and criticize someone negatively. A negative criticism would be calling someone stupid; idiot, retard, or you will never be anything in life. Positive criticism is maybe you need a little help, if you cannot do it know maybe practice to get better; patience is a virtue so few have. To understand this we must grasp what we try to hide away and that is the ability to rise above it all! Nothing is more important than do be criticized and criticize. As you grow and take learn to take good positive criticism you will be able to help other and be critical of them helping them to live wholes lives. Meaning can be lost in translation entirely, but it does not have to. Life is what we learn and reference to what we know. As I said previously Philosophers like Socrates, Plato, Aristotle, most resent philosophers of modern day tried to define this very lesson, but fell short. Greek philosophers may have created models to answer this being critical of one-self. Evan in Augustine finding of the true purpose of life it still leaves room for criticism review. Understanding this we come to the intricate knowledge of wholeness.

Modern Psychiatry would agree with me on this thesis of human reason and understanding of the Philosophical point that criticism is both positive and negative. Rather criticism in our lives is positive or negative they needed to grow truly. This was my hardest lesson, but when I understood it, it made a big difference in how I saw myself. The key to wholeness is the ability to receive and give criticism!

Dear Lord I live in fear and self-doubt. Help me to find the key to wholeness. Please give me the key to unlock the wisdom that comes from you "O" Lord. Take my fears and doubts and turn them to peace and rest. Give me the grace daily to handle every new day as a new adventure. I come to you whole-heartedly on my knees in prayer to search for answers for my tortured brain. Open up the floodgates of your mercy and let it rain down on me. Awaken my senses so that I can grow to become a shining example for others to follow. Help me to choose the *pilgrimage toward recovery* no–matter how hard it might be. Amen!

Chapter IV

Genesis of Chaos

By genesis of chaos, I am referring to the literal sense of going back to the beginning where we find that first bad remark or event we have hid away. That is where we are finding the key to our recovery. Why hide things away? We only betray our recovery needed in order to function! The things you hide away I am challenging you to bring to the service and deal them head on. Hiding your problems away in a closet of sorts is the way we avoid the harshness of some of our painful memories.

I heard it once said that one could not be wise unless we suffer much! For in suffering we gain wisdom. Dealing with the past, the many trials we endure develop character in us. The character we develop guides us through life, helping us to be an example for others in the same predicament as ourselves. What might seem chaotic to some might just be the light you need to guide you. Do not live with fear and trembling! *Let go! Take the hand of God an*d let God clean up your chaotic past. "For God is not a God of disorder, but of peace." (1Corinthians 14:33) I cannot see any reason why you will not let clean up your chaotic past. We wail and complain how we want to change, but we are not willing to go face to face with the chaos in our lives! "Cast all your anxieties on Him, because He cares for you." (1Peter 5:7) Jesus faced anxiety at Gethsemane and on the cross. At Gethsemane when Jesus prayed, He had the burden of all the sins of the world past, present, and future put upon his shoulders. On the cross, Jesus died with the burden of our sins weighing on his heart. Make the effort to change by relying on Jesus you will not regret it. For in our weakness Jesus shines through like a beacon of hope for others to see and share. People see us as frail, beaten down coming out of the fire unscathed. This in turn will encourage others around us to lean on the Holy Spirit with us and not on their own understanding making everything fall into place. Many of make excuses of why we cannot get control of our feelings, but you are only lying to yourself and stunting your own personal and spiritual growth. Why be stuck in our mental illness when we can be lifted up in glory? Simply we are afraid, but fear does not have to run our lives. Come on step out in faith my fellow pilgrim and you will be better off for it.

My own predicament started when my father said harsh words, one that I remember most sticking with me was I wish I never had a retard for a son. It is illegitimate to think neurosis is because of self-deceit being involved, but also giving light to the matter, we have a great deal to learn. It is only in coming to an existential self-awareness that we discover true neurosis empathy, because we gain nothing and learn absolutely nothing only impeding are learning. Do not let your neurotic suffering run your life, but take charge and move on. Remember the movie "What about Bob where Bill Murray played an Obsessive Compulsive person and Richard Dryfus played a psychiatrist who came up with a treatment called baby steps. Bill Murray's character follows his psychiatrist on vacation and through a series of funny interludes; the Obsessive Compulsive (Bill Murray) drives the psychiatrist insane. The psychiatrist (Richard Dryfus) tapes dynamite to Obsessive Compulsive (Bill Murray) back as what he calls shock therapy, but it back fires and Bill Murray's character gets the credit writing a book. This works with us, but it take some work on our behalf. We must take baby steps into the unknown of neurosis recovery. We find the source of true growth when we come to grips with our recovery. Like Richard Dryfus, we may all have our point of communication breakdown, but unlike his character we can come out of it with are head on straight. "He who ignores discipline denies himself, but whoever heeds correction gains understanding. The fear of the Lord teaches a man and humility comes before honor. (Proverbs 15:32-33)

This verse in Proverbs comes full circle in our understanding, because stopping the fear of the unknown leads to a healthy reverence of God. Affection is an acute sense that our willingness to show affection make us unique. God wants us to be humble servant willing to let Him show His love through us as His instruments in the orchristra of life. If you are not you than we do not know you. The world is missing out on your experience, so choose to be the you, your ment to be so that the world may benifit from your wisdom. We all have a story that can help someone on the pilgrimage toward recovery. If we grasp this concept then dealing with depression can be made ealier. Meditate on these and making it a daily routine. You are probably doing something about your mental development or have done some studying. You have read, thought, learned, and followed some calling hoping to become efficient in using your minds in some direction. If that is all, you are going to be; after all; only a lop-sided person's body and mind do not make up the whole personality. There is a mysterious or "three sides to the coin" as you find your spiritual nature. The true nature you have built inside you is a strange and subtle longing to discover the unseen and the infinite, because of this nature you sometimes know that the things, which you do not see are handled, are not enough for you. The simplest way of expressing that fact is by saying, deep down in you, you have a capacity for knowing a loving God and that until that capacity is satisfied you will never be at rest.

True health and recovery comes when we accept our mental limitations not as something bad, but what we learn from therm. Our main goal should be a day to day recovery. Let it be said, we recover we have a daily balance of learning and growing. Every day we must take a step forward in the *pilgrimage toward recovery*. Take each experience and let it be hope and virtue that you gain peace and serenity. Hope and peace comes in our ability to ourselves through how we love others. A great awakening out of the norm and mundane can get inspired to distance yourself from your daily routines changing them up a little to grow and move on. This said I might interject that this is just as easily thought as something to do than to actually do, we often let things like depression come in between are need to recover and for such a thing we make excuses. However, if you make recovery a priority, it is not hard to live outside ourselves and take some time to pray and get inspired. As a person writing this book, I have developed creative way to reboot the brain on overload and have more often than others.

Do you know how your love growth symptoms? Life is not always clear—cut sometimes making us frustrated not noticing that things need to change and upon this revelation love begins to build on the inside. As the grass is begins to go from yellow to green and living. Soon these trees will bud and the tulips will come up from the ground ready to make some changes in spring. Our life is like spring as I love myself and people love me. I put it out there for others to see wants to make some personal changes in hopes that we could encourage each other in the process. How do we change that simply by creating optomistic out look. To do this we cry out to Jesus and ask for his help and he will guide us. Let's think of it as taking a bath! When we take a bath we get clean ourselves in the bath. When we allow Jesus he will clean up the past and throw away the oldman. God will replace the oldman with newman. If we as peoples, who suffer with mental illness, put this into practice, we would crucify the negative attitudes of the past and learn new positive attitudes. Our old man has been done away with, and the new man begins to change in our lives.

We can begin to find cues when we start to understand the redundancy of a person's speech. What seems like nonsense to you might be important to the one speaking. People, who are redundant, tend to speak that way to hide the truth, because the truth hurts too much. The cue is then learned by understand the other person and when we do this we find ways to communicate. If we promise a person that, they could feel better for opening up. I sometimes do not communicate with my wife and she gets frustrated. Holding back verbal communication is something we all do, but not always a good thing when speaking to someone who is trying to help us. Cues play a crucial part in our *pilgrimage toward recovery*, because we need encouragement. If God gave me the choice to have healing, or left with my weaknesses, I would choose instead not to have a healing, because God can show His strength through my weakness. God has shown me many things in my hour of disappear to use to help other. One thing that stays with me is to trust him and he will come through. I still get overwhelmed and worry, but God always comes through on time. No matter what our circumstances might be, we can always depend on Jesus to be there. When we are at our weakest moments, Jesus is carrying us in his arms. Jesus says he will never leave us that he will always be by our side. It gives me comfort to know that my best friend is the God who created the universe. In compassing the mind, we also need to know the direction of need to know when to trash bad memories and when to hold onto them. A good word of advice is that when need to throw out the past is when they have been forgiven and done away with; You hold onto them when there are still issues need to get or ask forgiveness.

I always liked that line in "Forest Gump" when Forest says, "My momma always said life is; Like, a box of chocolates, you never know what you're going to get." Life tends to throw many unfortunate things at us and we cannot let them get us down, we need to gain strength from them. We do this by in compassing the mind, gaining excess to those things we buried in the dark regions of our mind. This is not always an easy process, because there is a lot of sacrifice of one's pride. As I will show you next, there is skill can be learned. If we can grasp this in during our *pilgrimage toward recovery,* depression will become more bearable. True mental health and recovery occurs when we accept our mental limitations and receive from them what we need to learn. Our daily goal should be a day-to-day recovery striving for a more manageable living circumstance! Learn something new every time you do something new, become in everything there is a lesson to learn. Stop saying, "I can't do this, and I can't do that". Just say, "I can do it." Saying yes to going to college is something new for me. I know there are moments when I think I am not good enough and that thought alone can stop me from continuing on, but by saying "I can do it and be able to follow through with a goal which is to finish college getting a degree as a Pastoral Psychologist.

Everyday take a baby step forward in this *pilgrimage toward recovery* taking each circumstance counting it as lesson in hope and peace grounded in the truth. Genuinely loving people are by definition people growing along with recovery. True love and nurturing is a product of the loving parents who taught this to the child at an early age. If we grasp this crucial point, dealing with depression made that much easier. Meditate on these things and make them a daily routine in your life. True mental health only comes when we begin to accept our mental limitations and receive from such limitations what we might learn about ourselves. Our lifetime goal should be a daily devotion devoted to recovery. Not every day we should start taking a great leap forward into the unknown, will never gain anything if we do not. Hope and peace come only when we truly know how to love others and ourselves. Dr. M. Scott Peck said on the topic of love, "Genuinely loving people by definition are growing people. I have spoken about how the capacity to love nurtured by parents, but I also noted that parental nurturing above fails to account the existence of the capacity in all people. Thus, I have come to believe peoples capacity to love, hence their will to grow, is nurtured only during childhood by loving parents, but also throughout their life by the grace of God's love." (Peck, 1979)

The Genesis of chaos is the rediscovey of our past in a different light, being showing and receiving genuine love. If our parents failed to show us mature genuine love then it is up to us to discovery it. Our parental parenting may not have been nurturing failing in all accounts loosing the existence or the capacity to love. You will come believe that people capacity to love starts at home. The ability to grow only nurtured, during childhood by loving parents and throughout their life by the grace of God's genuine love. The redirecting of the genesis of chaos is the key to which we are, so please take this heart and make it a daily part of your life. If this life throws you, unfortunate curves from time to time do not let them get you depressed, but gain strength from them. Compassing the mind, we to gain full excess to the junk buried in the dark regions of our mind. This is not an easy process for you to do. There is a lot of sacrifice that comes with it on our part. Here my hope that you can grasp this during your *pilgrimage toward recovery,* depression will become more bearable for you.

Finding the true, you sometimes might take dealing with the hurt what I referred to as the Genesis of Chaos. In this understanding, I am asking you to deal with the problem directly as they say and run with it. By running with it, I am asking you to deal with what you have hidden long enough. Find what made you feel the way you did when you were hurt negatively. This becomes your starting point in which you will work from to gain your recovery. This may be the hardest lesson you ever have to learn, because you have to deal with the past finally! Taking this step you will gain peace of mind I promise you that! **2Corinthians 2:6-10** "Sufficient to such a man is this punishment, which was inflicted of many. So that contrariwise ye *ought* rather to forgive *him,* and comfort him, lest perhaps such as one should swallow up with overmuch sorrow. Wherefore I beseech you that ye would confirm your love toward him. For to this end also did I write, that I might know the proof of you, whether ye are obedient in all things. To whom ye forgive anything, I forgive also: for if I forgave anything, to whom I forgave it, for your sakes forgave I sin in the person of Christ." In the realm of recover this scripture is vital to healing, knowing that God will heal us. God is in the business of healing and any time you call out to Him He is there with a healing touch. Life does not have to be as hard as we make out to be! This is a way out of this trauma and His name is Jesus Christ.

Dear lord heal me from the genesis of chaos in my life. Help me with my suffering and guide me. Let me discover the truth in discipline. As I grow, walk with me and lift me up. Help me come to grips with my genesis of chaos. Help me come to a closer walk with Thee. Give me strength to take baby steps in dealing with my neurotic behavior

Chapter V

Tools to Recovery

What are the tools to Recovery? They are the precepts we will use through our recovery. The first set of tools are found in **Galatians 5:22-23** "But the fruit of the Spirit is love, joy, peace, longsuffering, gentleness, goodness, faith, meekness, temperance: against such there is no law." I will show you how each one of these fruits of the spirit can become tools for your recover. Unquestionably, our self-images based on the undeniable fact that a good impression of us leads to success and success leads to happiness of the individual.

(1) Love: Does a calling to love God and love ourselves in return love others as well. It is important to love ourselves, because God first loved us. By learning too genuinely love yourself, you become unique and in doing, so you build the foundation in which you are to succeed. Love is the certification of all things and the sooner you grasp this the better you will feel.

(2) Joy: We must learn to receive and give joy as Jesus Christ did by dying so that we could have joy. Joy comes from understanding God and His love for us. God is exceedingly and overjoyed when we accept Him! **Zephaniah 3:17** "The LORD thy God in the midst of thee is mighty; he will save, he will rejoice over thee with joy; he will rest in his love, he will joy over thee with singing." If God can show us this much joy even with our flaws, certainly we can love and accept ourselves as God does. As we receive the Joy from the Lord, we pass it on to others and that is how we begin to recover.

(3) Peace: Peace comes out of praise and worship of our Mighty Creator. Praise Him for the wonderful you that He made and the work He is continuing in you. In this way, peace will fall on you as if a morning dove! True acceptance on Jesus is what begins the flow of peace and as we pass it on, we grow. Accepting Jesus, we become partners of a New Covenant with Jesus as the Prince of Peace giving us everlasting peace. In addition, this peace comes to live inside you and me!

(4) Patients: Patients is probably the most difficult one, it is developmental process through hard times. **James 1:1-4** "James, a servant of God and of the Lord Jesus Christ, to the twelve tribes which are scattered abroad, greeting. My brethren, count it all joy when ye fall into diverse temptations; knowing this, that the trying of your faith

worketh patience; but let patience have her perfect work, that ye may be perfect and entire, wanting nothing." I have a saying that I often say, "Patients is a virtue that so few have", cause when we learn the art of patient perseverance we begin to grasp patients and we have made a great leap forward.

(5) Kindness: Kindness can be a learning process as well, and if we are kind to others, it begins to rub off on us. How is this true? When you show kindness, making a person smile you should feel a sense of accomplishment. I am right about this, because when you show kindness you set yourself up to be free from bitterness that is like prison of your spirit. Never take for granted the size or shape of your deed, the only mistake is not taking a chance in the first place.

(6) Goodness: Goodness breaks the bonds that hold us down and this happens upon doing random acts of Goodness for strangers and close love-ones. By doing this, you can be blessed with an overwhelming amount of grace purifying the heart, mind, body, and spirit. It is a commonly known fact that when we help others it brings inner strength to our spirit. The people we help may one day become the very hope for our own recovery! How can this be? Doing good deeds for one person goes full circle and like a boomer-, range comes back to you. It is the concept of sowing and reaping coming into full term to the extent of its meaning.

(7) Faithfulness: This is the key, because our faith is our strength. With faith, we can move the *Mountain of Depression*. In faith, we stand tall in the valley of despair and such faith becomes the light at the end of the tunnel. Faith is the only way to find the only meaning in true recovery. Faith causes us to pray and prayer shapes us and molds us into a *person of purpose* ready to conquer the world. It is an all right thing to have faith! You ever heard the saying there are no atheist in foxholes? The only difference between a person of faith and Secularist is people of religious persuasion have hope in a loving God.

(8) Gentleness: With gentleness come reason and wisdom, because in light of it

We begin to listen in a completely new way. A gentle spirit is giving and being gentle to one another develops a renewed and refreshed spirit.

41

Living with a gentle heart will refresh your soul and renew your mind. God implores the gentle heart with gifts of grace. At times, it is hard to be of gentle heart, but it the key to recovery in the sense that you do not carry around a heavy heart.

(9) Self-control: Upon developing self-control, we begin to shape our character and self-worth. Such character helps us to understand what we do not know or fear to know. Self-control helps us find value and purpose in our own recovery. God made you just how you are and He sees you as a purposeful person, so do not give up on yourself God has not. Hold your confidence high knowing that God has created a purpose just for you and you alone!

With the fruit of the spirit is being used as tools for recovery, it sheds some light on the process of personal recovery. Each tool shows us more about ourselves in the way we reflect in relationships with our friends, family, and Jesus Christ. Why continue to live in a constant state of depression? We have the necessary tools to recover, so go ahead, and develop them into our lives. As these tools develop in us, we start helping others and ourselves. As a person in recovery, we have been so hurt that we need an experience of someone else being able to love us unconditionally before we can love again including ourselves. Therapy based on a relationship, trust, mutual support, and guidance making our efforts worth examining bringing us to a place of letting go of self-putting our hope in positive beliefs. Take regard for therapy that or the thought as the means to giving you the greatest gift of all, learning to love yourself!

Now let us talk about the tools of our warfare, because we are going to battles many demons from our past and we need to know how to deal with them. **Ephesians 6:10-17** "Finally, my brethren, be strong in the Lord, and in the power of his might. Put armor of God that ye may be able to stand against the wiles of the devil. For we wrestle not against flesh and blood, but against principalities, against powers, against the rulers of the darkness of this world, against spiritual wickedness in high places. Wherefore take unto you the whole armor of God that ye may be able to withstand in the evil day, and having done all, to stand. Stand therefore, having your loins girt about with truth, and having on the breastplate of righteousness; And your feet shod with the preparation of the gospel of peace; Above all, taking the shield of faith, wherewith ye shall be able to quench all the fiery darts of the wicked. And take the helmet of salvation and the sword of the Spirit, which is the word of God" Believe me knowing these safeguards will come in handy down the road. This should be a prayer when you first wake up in the morning and throughout your days, as you need it. Your recovery from mental illness is the key in this *pilgrimage toward recovery*.

Belt of Truth: The belt would hold the kilt and breastplate in place along with a sheaf for sword, a common wear of any Centurion Guard. In like aspect, the belt should be our premise of truth holding our faith to the principles of God. This was we keep our faith ready for when we need it during those times when we become depressed with negative thoughts plague our minds. With the proper definition of truth in our lives, we find the means to live.

Breastplate of Righteousness: The breastplate would protect the Centurion Guard from piercing arrows way that come his direction. In like manor for the breastplate of righteousness protects the heart of the spirit-man from emotional wounds. In one sense, it protects the very heart of faith. This gives God the ability to mold and shape us into what he wants us to be.

Shoes of Truth: The shoes of the Centurions would be made of strong leather straps and very think soles giving the Centurion Guard the stand his ground while under attack. In like aspect, the shoes of truth should give a firm place to stand. They set o feet on the rock of Christ Jesus steadying our walk while facing the storms of negative thought that plague us. They give us a firm well-grounded stance in our *pilgrimage toward recovery*.

Shield of Faith: The shield for the Centurion is steel pressed with tightly fastened leather stretched in place. This would help block most arrows that shoot in his direction extinguishing them. In like aspect, the shield of faith should be our weapon to extinguish the arrows of negativity. This also builds our self-confidence to live out our faith with a renewed sense of purpose.

Helmet of Salvation: For the Centurion Guard this made of mixture of steel and iron giving him protection to his head. This helmet would protect him from fatal blows while in battle. In like aspect, the helmet of salvation keeps the devil from constantly plaguing our minds with negative thoughts. With this in place, we can start control of our minds allowing us a period of rest.

Sword of the Spirit: The sword for the Centurion was heat tempered steel usually sharp enough to cut through bone as well as flesh. The Centurion well trained in how to use his sword. In comparison in like aspect, we must train ourselves in God's Word, so that we become warriors of righteousness. The more we know the Word of God the better equipped we will be in our *pilgrimage toward recovery*. The Sword of the Spirit (the Word of God) should become our weapon of choice to use against the negative thoughts. You quote back scripture at the Devil and he will coward away.

These tools should help you grasp true recovery and spiritual health and growth. I solemnly believe we can have peace and rest in our tormented lives. Just as depression can affect your health, so can the tools affect you positively. I never said the *pilgrimage toward recovery* was going to be an easy one, but these tools can make it easier to manage. Practice these tools and you will start to see recovery in a completely new way in your daily lives. I still fall into bouts of depression, but these tools help me get back up. Using these tools properly will not only give you the means to battle negative thoughts, but you turn the negative thoughts around to positive thoughts. When you utilize the tools Jesus Christ will give, you back dignity. Remember God delights in us and He gives these tools freely. So use them wisely in the *pilgrimage toward recovery*. There is a great deal of ignorance, confusion, and fear in Christian circles surrounding this issue and these tools help us through. Christians in the past have been quick to judge depression and other types of mental illness for a weak faith or satanic influence, but that think with the use of the tools discussed in this chapter we can influence the same Christian communities with the truth. Christian communities need to understand clinical depression, bipolar disorder or other mental illnesses for what it is and accept Christ. The taboo about mental illness is understandable, to an extent—anyone who has lived through serious depression or knows that it's a harrowing experience to here inspirational stories or resolutions of recovery. One can only wonder if the church's difficulty with the issue has its roots in a mixed t up doctrine. Tools discuss this far should ignite us to stand our ground educate the people whom just do not understand.

Dear Lord at times, I feel lost at sea with no land in sight. I feel I know myself anymore. Help me apply these tools to my life and give me strength in the battle for my salinity. Show me how to use the weapons of our warfare. Yes, Lord I want victory in my life! I thank you in advance for victory!

Amen!

Chapter VI

The Unspoken Taboo

The unspoken taboo is suicide or suicidal thoughts. We all face this in our *pilgrimage toward recovery* to be whole. Most people shun suicide as if it is you should never be talk about let alone mentioned in civil society. If left alone unselective suicide becomes a deadly killer that affects many experiencing great emotional loss for those left. In my own *pilgrimage toward recovery*, I have had suicidal thought plague my mind, but the Lord Jesus Christ gives me grace to keep on pushing onward. Believe me when I say suicide is only a cop-out to and not the answer! This might be hard for some to accept, but it is ultimately the truth. If all live by a Philosophical or Judeo Christian moral code then we would have to accept that suicide is just morally wrong. It the ones we love by making them feel like they were of no help to us.

Dr. M. Scott Peck says there is a moral code of ethics we all live by and it is not right to life not even your own. "Code of ethics is of situational ethics. The Ten Commandments our example of ancient ethic and declare certain acts as being wrong in of themselves regardless of situation. The Sixth Commandment for instants states flatly: "Thou shall not kill!" It does not say thou shall not kill except a Philistine; thou shall not kill except in self-defense. I say thou shall not kill, period!" (Peck, 1993) I understand life can be unbearable sometimes, but there is always a way out. Do not take what God has given and misuse it by not use it. You can phrase this as a choice in so many different ways. One person may say it is choice to be co-being with God and others say it is our choice to love. Choosing genuine—love we choose a life-long criticism and discipline, but it will stretch out beyond your means inevitably developing your spirit into a united spirit with God.

Pilgrim choose to follow Jesus Christ and your life will not be the same! **Psalm 23** "The LORD *is* my shepherd; I shall not want. He maketh me to lie down in green pastures: he leadeth me beside the still waters. He restoreth my soul: he leadeth me in the paths of righteousness for his name's sake. Yea, though I walk through the valley of the shadow of death, I will fear, no evil: for thou art with thy rod; thy staff and me, they comfort me. Thou preparest a table before me in the presence of mine enemies: thou anointest my head with oil; my cup runneth over. Surely goodness and mercy shall follow me all the days of my life: and I will dwell in the house of the LORD forever." Some people might argue that suicide is not mentioned in the Bible accept maybe once. I beg to differ; I found seven suicides in the Bible. Each suicide unique, six out of seven done out of selfish motives. Most of these suicides I found were committed, because the people in question did not want to face the consequences of their crimes. God would have forgiven these men if I only called upon Him.

(1) Abimelech: **Judges 9:50-55** "Then went Abimelech to Thebez, and encamped against Thebez, and took it. However, there was a strong tower within the city, and thither fled all the men and women, and all they of the city, and shut it to them, and gat them up to the top of the tower. In addition, Abimelech came unto the tower, fought against it, and went hard unto the door of the tower to burn it with fire. In addition, a certain woman cast a piece of a millstone upon Abimelech's head, and all to break his skull. Then he called hastily unto the young man his armourbearer, and said unto him, Draw thy sword, and slay me, that men say not of me, a woman slew him. In addition, his young man thrust him through, and he died. And when the men of Israel saw that Abimelech was dead, they departed every man unto his place." Here you see a ruthless man who did not want to die knowing it would be in the hands of woman. Not only did he die by the hands of a woman, but lost the battle and could not accept defeat.

(2) Samson: **Judges 16:28-31** And Samson called unto the LORD, and said, O Lord GOD, remember me, I pray thee, and strengthen me, I pray thee, only this once, O God, that I may be at once avenged of the Philistines for my two eyes. In addition, Samson took hold of the two middle pillars upon which the house stood, and on which it was borne up, of the one with his right hand, and of the other with his left. In addition, Samson said, let me die with the Philistines. In addition, he bowed himself with all his might; and the house fell upon the lords, and upon all the people that *were* therein. Therefore, the dead, which he slew at his death, were more than they, *which* he slew in his life. Then his brethren and all the house of his father came down, took him, brought him up, and buried him between Zorah and Eshtaol in the burying place of Manoah his father. And

he judged Israel twenty years." For argument sake let say that this could be the only suicide that a man went to Heaven. God used this apparent suicide to bring wrath down on the Philistines. Moreover, the fact that Samson pleaded for his life before killing himself.

(3) Saul: **1Samuel 31:3-4** "And the battle went sore against Saul, and the archers hit him; and he was sore wounded of the archers. Then said Saul unto his armourbearer, Draw thy sword, and thrust me through therewith; lest these uncircumcised come and thrust me through, and abuse me; But his armourbearer would not; for he was sore afraid; Therefore Saul took a sword, and fell upon it." Saul was a king who rejected by God and would not accept stepping down to younger man named David. It did not help that David spared Saul's life three times. While in battle, fighting against the Philistines Saul overtaken and instead of calling on God, he selfishly took his own life.

(4) Saul's Armbearer: **1Saul 31:5-6** "And when his armourbearer saw that Saul was dead, he fell likewise upon his sword, and died with him. So Saul died, and his three sons, and his armourbearer, and all his men, that same day together." Saul's Armbearer is simply a matter of unmerited, giving into the fear of the overwhelming presence of Philistine Army. Instead of believing in God for his deliverance, he took matters into his own hands and killed himself.

(5) Ahithophel: **2Samuel 17:23** "And when Ahithophel saw that his counsel was not followed, he saddled his ass, and arose, and gat him home to his house, to his city, and put his household in order, and hanged himself, and died, and was buried in the sepulchre of his father." Not this was a classic pity routine where Ahithophel gave bad advice to capture David and he thought David would never forgive him. I believe that if Ahithophel went to David would have forgiven him, because he was David's best friend and most important advisor.

(6) Zirmri: **1Kings 16:17-18** "At the end of Zirmri's rein Omri went up from Gibbethon, all Israel with him, and besieged Tirzah. And it came to pass, when Zimri saw that the city was taken, that he went into the palace of the king's house, and burnt the king's house over him with fire, and died." Zirmri was another example on how

pride befalls a man. Zirmri killed the king and his family and made himself king and when discovered he took his own life with no remorse.

(7) Judas: **Matthew 27:3–5** "Then Judas, which had betrayed him, when he saw that he was condemned, repented himself, and brought again the thirty pieces of silver to the chief priests and elders; Saying, I have sinned in that I have betrayed the innocent blood. In addition, they said, what is that to us? See thou to that. Then he cast down the pieces of silver in the temple, and departed, and went and hanged himself." Now Judas could have asked Jesus to forgive him and I believe that Jesus would have. Judas consumed with fear and guilt regretting what he had done. I love the scene in the in the Passion where it showed demons tormenting Judas driving him mad until his final act of suicide was done.

Dr M. Scott Peck makes the point clear dealing with free-will, free choice and the morality issue. "As creatures of free will we have the power to kill ourselves. Weather we have the moral or ethical right to do so is a different matter entirely. However, act of re one sets the timing of his death without reverence to the Life-Giver. It is a denial of God and His relationship with our soul." (Peck, 1993) When God said we our wonderfully made, why would we want to kill ourselves? We should run not walk toward the source of our hope, God! God can give us the grace we need to through our current dilemma. Nothing in life is really, that bad!

I know it is not easy, because of those moments of depression when all hope seems lost. At those times, we need to seek a Psychiatrist, Pastor, Councilor or friend for help in coping. From time to time, we all need a Psychiatrist it is OK! Even the ones who we consider stronger than ourselves need help, though they will not admit it. The love we experience in life is too strong to give up. Just tap into the love of God, the means for survival. **Zephaniah 3:17** "The LORD thy God in the midst of thee is mighty; he will save, he will rejoice over thee with joy; he will rest in his love, he will joy over thee with singing." Wow, is not that awesome to think about! Does that mean us who are suicidal as well? The answer is yes, because what God said he would do for the Israelites genially refers to us as Christians. God has adopted into the blessing of Israel by the cleansing blood of Christ as believers.

Meditate on Zephaniah 3:14-17, believing it as if God is talking to you personally. "Genially speaking there are always exceptions it is the chronicity of emotional pain that properly determines when and rather we need medical attention." (Peck, 1993) What Dr. M. Scott Peck says is so true in dealing with the fact at hand, which is the state of mind we are feeling. Most of the time what we are feeling is a figment of the mind due to a delayed response to a negative outside source.

I believe personally that some of us need medicines to help u with the physical aspects of depression, but God can heal the underlining cause. If you are reading this book and are suicidal, please read on give the Almighty God a chance and I. I know you will not regret it, because I have been there myself and I know what you are facing right now. This can be a real lonely world when you are depressed and feeling all alone. If you take the plunge into the darkness of suicide, you do not only hurt yourself, but the people who love you and care about you. God is always there he will talk to through the Word of God (the Bible).

The current state of mind that you might be in at this moment does not merit us the right to take our own life. That choice belongs to God and He is powerful enough to bring us through the hardship. The mind can be a wicked monster if we let, so we need to train our minds to respond to God and not the fear that creeps up from time to time. Life has so much to offer if we only take time to smell the roses. We are created by God to be people of purpose and until we discover our purpose, we can never escape the web of suicide that lurks around every corner.

Dear Lord, I am falling on my way to becoming a statistic among those who commit suicide. People will refer to me has an unspoken taboo (something spoke in secret). I feel trapped in the forest and the shadow that it cast. Hear my cry "O" Lord, my desperate plea for help! Please Lord become my guide and showeth me to the light peace. Take my brokenness and replace it with "Your" grace. Showeth me grace that passes all understanding that I may find my self-worth in "You" and forgive me for every for every negative thought that I had that nailed "You" to the cross. Take this frail and broken body and make me a new creation in Christ Jesus!

Chapter VII

Recovery in Progress

We are a recovery in progress learning as we travel down this *pilgrimage toward recovery.* As I mentioned in previous chapters recovery is a lifelong journey. We need to take control of our mind and our spirit. How we do that you ask? It takes a willingness to suffer through anguish taking it to the limits of time getting to know your-self through the emotional pain and becoming a friend to that emotional pain. **Psalm 18:5-6** "The sorrows of hell compassed me about: the snares of death prevented me. In my distress I called upon the LORD, and cried unto my God: he heard my voice out of his temple, and my cry came before him, even into his ears." If and God is this Psalm is true e and God is with us, then we should have no problem asking Him to fulfill our lifelong dream of recovery. There is an old wise saying that you are what you say you are. A successful purposeful person follows their dreams until there fulfilled. I would never ask you to abandon others in the fulfillment of your dream of recovery, but I will ask you to seek the benefit of others to help you discover your expectations of yourself. By learning to dwell on the positive, your life will move toward the right direction every time, but dwell on the negative and you will get off course. A lesson I struggle with everyday and still learning, but I am getting better!

Negativity only leads to failure or mediocrity ultimately leading too sabotage of this stage in recovery with any attempt for better than average performance. That is why I must tell you this; the key element to true recovery is having vision expectancy over the negative state of consciousness you are in by raising the bar. A positive mind endures all hardships, but a negative mind fails at every obstacle. Change what society has taught you and wrong prove them all by becoming a *Pilgrim toward Recovery* full of purpose and hope. Think about this concept for moment and you can see that my reasoning is true in form. In understanding this, we must think rationally and reason analytically by self-diagnosis of our mind and spirit.

Jeremiah in the Old Testament did his own analytical thinking, self-diagnosing, and finding a battle cry for Israel. **Jeremiah 4:19** "Oh my anguish, my anguish I writhe in pain. Oh the agony of my heart my heart pounds within me, I cannot keep silent. For I have heard the sound of the trumpet; I have heard the battle cry." {NIV} 'O' Lord I am in agony from my self-made prison of negativity, give me means to escape, your anxiety and anguish, so why do we need to feel where alone? At a place called Gethsemane Jesus wept tears of blood. **Luke 22:42-44** ""Father, if you are willing, take this cup from me; yet not my will, but yours be done." An angel from heaven appeared to him and strengthened him. And being in anguish, he prayed more earnestly, and his sweat was like drops of blood falling to the ground." Jesus gives us an awesome example when faced with moments of anxiety. Do not let these be the times when you do not feel like talking to anyone, but just reach out to Christ the way he reached out to his Heavenly Father praying wholeheartedly. Put down the selfish-pity-pride and reach out to a fellow *Pilgrim toward Recovery*, you will not regret you did. This should be an inspiring thought, to motivate you to find support from church family or counseling group. It is a good thing to take advice from others as well as give advice to other *Pilgrims toward Recovery*. If someone asked you were crazy you say know I am a *pilgrim in recovery*! Take hope in the fact that you have chosen this *self-recovery pilgrimage* in this moment in time. Jesus Christ by his own sacrifice took our sins upon himself on a cross and he will help us to break our will, so that we might become whole in God.

Learning to take a moment to breathe is like loving and loving freely. In moments such as these, it is wise to be quiet and still and rest in the security of God. Isaiah 30:15 "This is what the Sovereign LORD, the Holy One of Israel, says: "In repentance and rest is your salvation, in quietness and trust is your strength, but you would have none of it." (NIV) Better yet in times such times as this God puts a sudden urge upon our hearts to be still in His holy presence. He does this so that we can recovery our fragile state of mind. I know that our recovery process is hard and some days we feel like, "throwing in the towel". Let me please interject a hopeful thought, the fact that God considered worthy. If the Creator of the Universe sees us as being worthy, why do we see ourselves as worthy? We can rise up to a higher standard for ourselves and make our life more manageable. Reach out to the Lord Almighty and quench your thirst for acceptance.

Song of Solomon 8:7 "Many waters cannot quench love; rivers cannot wash it away. If one were to give all the wealth of his house for love, it would be utterly scorned." God will open doors for us and He will give spiritual wealth. God will give us an ever-flowing supply of grace that will never run dry. Most recovering pilgrims ask, what is my purpose in God's plan for me? Does God really want me just the way I am? Does this life have a reason why I am in it? Next paragraph will answer these three questions.

Accept God made us the way we are for a much greater purpose! If we were not than others like us could never know Jesus Christ. We all need someone who understands even when we are broken and frail. Become that person for someone else and you will begin to change from within. Every moment has a reason and every reason crosses paths with honesty. That means to be honest with others and ourselves as well. "They need not to waste any effort covering their tracks our main training disguises. An ultimately they will find that the energy required for self-discipline of honesty is far less than the energy required for secretiveness. The more honest we are the easier it is to continue to be honest, just as will more lies one has told that easier it would be to live again. By their openings, people dedicated to that true live in the open and through the exercise to their courage to live in the open, they become free from fear;" said Dr. M. Scott Peck (Peck, The Road Less Traveled, 1979)

When we live to ourselves, it is l like lying to our peers, because they never see the true you. It does not take much to dedicate your-self to the truth. That is the truth of oneself in light of the world around him. As pointed out why waste so much of our effort on been secret? We are only hurting ourselves in the long term of things. Use the energy four leading in the truth to your-self and being open with others. You will only grow out of the experience! Just like wasteful energy taking to frown, it takes less energy to smile. Come on, turn your life around for the better and smile. Take a gamble you will not regret! "Many people are insecure about who they are, so they constantly trying to gain approval of everybody all around them, so they can feel better about themselves. They end up living to please other people, trying to fit into their models so that they can be accepted. They act one way for their boss, another way for their spouse and another way for their friends. They live a life of pretence, wearing various masks and happy to please everybody. In essence they are not being true to anyone, especially themselves."

(Osteen, 2004) In our own recovery, a person who is truthful to others and his self is a purposeful person.

To be truthfully honest we must find peace and peace can come in some of the most unexpected places. Peace can come in a song, a baby's cry, a friendly smile or kind word. All the answers in our *pilgrimage toward recovery* found in the face of love. When you have nothing in life to cling to, God is for you. Draw closer in all that you do and everything else will fall into place. We need to stop limiting God with narrow-mindedness and self-less thinking. As *pilgrims in recovery*, we need to focus on what we can conceive and keep the image of what we want to be in front of our view. You will be able to heal and come all that you become what you believe that you will. God may tell you something in the natural realm that may seem imposable, but with God all things possible. Believe in God and praise him with every breath praising him for every blessing. Even thanking Him for the hardships, because He is getting us ready for something better.

Dear Lord I have chose to become a recovery in progress, so help me recover every day. Teach me to be a light for others who are in recovery. Help me to take off my masks. I want to be open and exposed to the Lord so that I can grow mentally, physically and spiritually. Take this broken vessel and make something of me. Put forth the image that you would like to go out to represent you. Create in me a clean heart that I might shine and be guide for recovery that others may follow. Amen!

Chapter VIII

Broken and Burntout

At times while in recovery, we feel broken and burnt-out and void of any feeling. The times that we are, broken God is molding and shape us into a vessel used by Him for the benefit of others. God takes great pleasure in His creation and will not despise even in our weakness. "The sacrifices of God are a broken spirit; a broken and contrite heart, O God, you will not despise." **Psalm 51:17** God will be with us even when we were are broken and frail. He will be close as a thought or a word. Just reach out to God and He will comfort you. **Psalm 38:18** "I confess my iniquity; I am troubled by my sin." He will meet you where you are and change into a new creation. **Psalm 147:3** "He heals the brokenhearted and binds up their wounds."

"It is no accident that I have relearned the art of crying, at thirty-six while I was in a true community setting. Despite this relearning my early rugged individualism was sufficiently affective that even today I cry in public only when in a safe place." (Dr. M. Scott Peck, 1987, p. 67) When we feel unable to cry let alone be safe this quote by Dr. M. Scott Peck plays a big part. By no means does this say a good cry is always the answer, but that it helps us to feel safe. Crying brings about hope and security and releases all the pain that we build up in our refusal to deal with abuse in our past. Mostly it can be said that God hears our cries and comforts us, because all our hope is found in Jesus Christ our Lord! "The Spirit of the Sovereign LORD is on me, because the LORD has anointed me to preach good news to the poor. He has sent me to bind up the brokenhearted, to proclaim freedom for the captives and release from darkness for the prisoners." (**Isaiah 61:1**) Jesus fulfilled this by healing the sick and comforting the broken hearted, so if He did this while Have was on earth how much more would who do being in heaven with God the Father. While in recovery, we need to paint a picture in our mind of an eagle soaring over the storm knowing that we are the eagle rising above our negative circumstances.

It is in those times when answers are not enough that we find hope. So by no means, throw in the towel and quit. "But those who hope in the LORD will renew their strength. They will soar on wings like eagles; they will run and not grow weary, they will walk and not be faint."(**Isaiah 40:31**) Know that you are not alone and escape come from waiting on God. Telling you negative thought about being alone is only the Devil trying to drag you down. True recovery comes from learning to depend on God u our peers. You find recovery when you accept predicaments for what they are, either a chemical imbalance in the brain or a circumstance that happened beyond our control. Learn to depend on God and others for true recovery. Recovery comes when we accept our predicaments for what they are, and that is an imbalance of the brain.

The imbalance can be genial, hormonal or chemical or all three. When we see as possible a limitation we can create ways to work around it. We can rise above our emotional problems if we try hard enough. I am living proof to this fact. By most standards I was considered retarded, but I beat the odds and built myself as a person of purpose. On paper, my IQ was or is 75 to 80, but I have succeeded too amazed people by doing what to some might seem impossible. Technically speaking I am a walking miracle. For someone like me to have held jobs for five years or more is an accomplishment. Another great accomplishment is being a published poet. My best accomplishment though is going to college being a B+ student, because of my learning disability. "Success is not defined by position or pay scale, but by this: Doing the most of what you do best." (Luccado, 2005, p. 43) I am doing what I do best and that is writing. I have decided to write this book for you the reader.

I can say with absolute assurance that there is hope for your future and the hope is found in being intimate relationship with God. **Proverbs 23:18** "There is surely a future hope for you, and your hope will not be cut off." You believe with all certainty that in the presence of God there is hope for a better tomorrow. In being face to face with God, we discover an efficient sense of value and self-worth. However, this may be a difficult *pilgrimage* to undertake, but I promise you it will be worth it. Tomorrow just might be the day of your self-discovery where you find true inner peace. Why live with a broken spirit when God is with you? Why forsake God, and what He made you to become? With the confidence of self-discovery, myself I can tell you that there is strength in self-discipline. For it is in discipline we find grace to handle all the emotional storms in life. Proverbs 23:19 "Listen, my son, and be wise, and keep your heart on the right path." As Solomon is telling his son can be applied to us on our *pilgrimage toward recover*. We will discover something fresh and find a true sense of self-worth and meaning in our lives. In this, we will discover our purpose by using our disability we were meant to help others with similar problems! It like the old wise saying of cause and effect governs every aspect of our lives, because it is the cause (our disability) having an effect (on others like us).

At the very moment, we become burnt-out remember their others out there like us going through the same thing as you. Just like you, they are on the same *pilgrimage toward recovery* trying find meaning, support and self-confidence. Confidence can only come when we accept our Mental Illness for what it is and that is an illness beyond our control. Can we be taught to do the unnatural, so how hard could it be to do the unnatural and go beyond ourselves? **Ecclesiastes 12:13** "Now all has been heard; here is the conclusion of the matter: Fear God and keep his commandment, for this is the whole duty of man. Find the benefit of human character and you will discover true worth. Do the will of God and everything fall into place as you live God will for your life! "The tendency to avoid challenges is so omnipresent in human beings that it can properly be considered a characteristic of human nature; but calling it natural does not mean it is essential, beneficial, or unchangeable behavior. It is also natural to defecate in our pants and never brush teeth. Yet we teach ourselves to do the unnatural until the unnatural becomes it-self second nature." (Peck, The Road Less Traveled, 1979, p. 53)

Solomon had done everything under the sun, so his conclusion should be reliable. Solomon suffered much and gained much, but at the end of his life, he realized that he had to get his heart right with God. We find our value in self-worth in the reverence of God! Purpose is an act of self-discovery, discovering your-self as if being loved by God. This may be hard for you to accept, but you do have a purpose for living. I dare you to search your-self and become a teacher to others. Believe me, you will find self-gratification when you teach others the tools needed to recover. For it is in our ability to think and think well that we help our-selves and others like us. Do not ever for a moment think you are a waste of time. You have a purpose for living and remember God loves you!

The Devil wants you to live a life full of depression, so you will govern your life by the label that the world puts on you. Many things, people and places I have experienced or observed throughout my life became familiar in aspect of failure. In recovery we seem to rate ourselves by the common error formula that was a learned response from childhood. Not thinking about the circumstance is to lose our-self preservation and only leads to our own self-destruction. Another thing we tend to do is making assumptions in thinking through with one-dimensional logic by giving and receiving stereotypes causing faulty labels. We can also fall into the warped belief that thinking and communication do not take much effort. Never assume that thinking and communicating is a waste of time, while dealing with a particular factor of our experience. Never except failure as the means of coping, its only illogical reasoning of solving problems that need to be solved. In our *pilgrimage toward recovery* to gain emotional health, it is a necessary logical factor to learn to grasp the logic of thinking.

Another avenue to look at is the act of fellowship where we find the ability to learn from them and them learning from us. When you are broken and burnt-out you cannot rely only on yourself, it only brings unnecessary suffering. True recover takes a lot of effort on our part. Take a good hard look at yourself and you can be guaranteed you will find within you a purposeful person. If you are depressed and anxiety as overtaken you, know this God takes great delight in you even in all your faults. God holds you up in high regard, so put all fragilities on Christ Jesus and have confidence in His plan for your life. Jeremiah 17:7 "But blessed is the man who trusts in the LORD, whose confidence is in him." Finding fellowship with other believers in the same predicament is a great way to find true meaning oneself. It is in such fellowship we learn the art of analyzing and analyze others in the process.

Doing the learning processes, we can grow in our recovery and have emotional health. Philippians 2:1 "If you have any encouragement from being united with Christ, if any comfort from his love, if any fellowship with the Spirit, if any tenderness and compassion, then make my joy complete by being like-minded, having the same love, being one in spirit and purpose. Do nothing out of selfish ambition or vain conceit, but in humility consider others better than your-selves. Each of you should look not only to your own interests, but also to the interests of others." This I hope can be some encouragement to you and brings you comfort. It is so true that being in one spirit brings a sense of purpose.

Dear Lord I am broken and burnt-out from suffering with my frail self. Take my suffering and give me peace and rest. I surrender all to you, so can take care of the rest. Come to me and teach me how to fellowship with others (my peers). Lord gives to me a sense of peace and purpose in life. Lord you are my lighthouse guiding me through life's many storms. Teach me Your, so I can teach others.

Chapter IX

Discipline of Grace

Grace derives from the Greek word gratos meaning to hit the mark, in reference to archery the mark being the red center dot. God gives of grace so that we can hit the mark all the time. The mark being the presence of God where long to be, a placed called home. It is awesome to think that the God who created everything would give us such a marvelous gift. God hails us and finds favor in his creation (us). These are great eternal truths for people like you and me to meditate on a daily basis. Jesus Christ paid the ransom for a dept that was not his and that is the wages of sin. Grace is a wonderful gift, so pass it on and share it with others you meet.

As good, as grace is it takes discipline to keep it in your life! As I said before this *pilgrimage toward recovery* was never going to be easy, that goes for grace as well. Yes! Grace is a free-gift from God, but comes with a lesson to be learned. The lesson that we must all grasp is discipline and once we grasp it we will better off for it. Grace is our help through the repercussions of blurred actions or mishaps. If grace is a gift, why must we work hard? Let me ask you this in reply, why should God give us anything when we fail? The answer is simple, because he loves us more than we can fathom in our tiny finite minds. "Discipline is meaning for solving life's problem. All discipline is a form of submission. The discipline to discern what we are or are not responsible is most crucial, sense we must go through the existential suffering of choosing when we and what we summit to; Whether that is our own ego, love, God and even forces of evil." (Peck, The Road Less Traveled and Beyond, 1997, pp. 147-148) If Dr. M. Scott Peck is right then I can assume that discipline and grace go hand in hand.

Grace without discipline becomes less effective and discipline without grace becomes less effective. Jesus shows us this example by washing his disciple's feet. John 13:5-15 "After that, he poured water into a basin and began to wash his disciples' feet, drying them with the towel that was wrapped around him. He came to Simon Peter, who said to him, "Lord, are you going to wash my feet?" Jesus replied, "You do not realize now what I am doing, but later you will understand." "No," said Peter, "you shall never wash my feet." Jesus answered, "Unless I wash you, you have no part with me." Then, Lord, Simon Peter replied, not just my feet but my hands and my head as well!" Jesus answered, "A person who has had a bath needs only to wash his feet; his whole body is clean. And you are clean, though not every one of you." For he knew who was going to betray him, and that was why he said not everyone was clean. When he had finished washing their feet, he put on his, clothes and returned to his place. "Do you understand what I have done for you?" he asked them. "You call me 'Teacher' and 'Lord,' and rightly so, for that is what I am. Now that I, your Lord and Teacher, have washed your feet, you also should wash one another's feet. I have set you an example that you should do as I have done for you."

Jesus was showing grace and discipline by giving the disciples an example of being a servant. He disciplined himself a stepped out of his position as Lord to become a servant. For us to truly recover than we must follow Christ example and become an example to others who struggle. Receive the gift and pass it on as a sacrifice to the God! In all aspects of the word, grace shows us a sense of delight when God see us through the love of Jesus Christ. **Song of Solomon 7:10** "I belong to my lover, and his desire is for me." **Song of Solomon 7:6** "How beautiful you are and how pleasing, O love, with your delights!" As these Bible verses of scripture imply, God shows endless grace and mercy. No matter where we are and how we feel, the Lord is near to heal and minister to us. God delights in giving us support. There is nothing to hard when God is with us. With grace, we are called to use wisdom, because we become committed to it.

I know that it is hard to break out of our comfort zone, but it is necessary in order to begin and or continue in the recovery process. This means that in grace we are called inform others of our own transformation. The Greek word is (gymutes): The lacking of divine nakedness, to cloth the soul. Another Greek word is (gnorzio) to make known, declare and reveal, tell inform or teach an accretion to find out. In our spiritual nakedness from anxiety, depression, stricken with fear we must become clothed with God and His grace. For our loving God comforts us in our weary times with His own tears. Believe me that He cries when we cry and laughs when we laugh! Our loving Father will encourage us to hang on when we are standing on the brink. If we only cry out to Him and wait, God will quietly, patiently and gently answer us, because He loves us to much to leave us in the pit.

Discipline is the teacher and grace is the comforter! Without discipline, how would we ever know grace? The answer lies in the fact that in our hour of need there is so much to learn, if we only open up our eyes. In the harshness of our anxiety, it is finding self-discovery in our mind and spirit is crucial. It is these times we need to seek God through His word, letting the Word continue to grow coming alive to give you hope for tomorrow. This is a growth process and needs to be done for our recovery. We fail to see discipline we fail to see a correct perception of the world around us. It becomes distorted in relating to a minds-eye-view of where we live. "As human-beings growing in discipline and love and life experiences, their understanding of the world and their experiences in it naturally grows apace. Conversely, as people fail to grow in discipline and love and life experiences, does their understanding, fail to grow." (Peck, The Road Less Traveled and Beyond, 1997, p. 185) We must allow discipline and grace to have their way in order to overcome our circumstances. By doing this we learn more about ourselves from the world around us, because we learn to understand ourselves through the eyes of others.

As my understanding of scripture goes, it is true that all answers to any problem can be found in the Bible. When on a *pilgrimage toward recovery* the Bible should be our main tool for recovery. It is an awesome thing to know that God walks with us, if we only step out of comfort zone. If we do not we can never grow into a purposeful person full of wisdom. Why live in the solitude of our mind? I know that most of us find comfort in such solitude, but I promise you that seeking after Jesus in the scripture will make it easier. When comes to understanding God and His Word, the grass is always greener on the other-side. Let me please tease you with a game of archery in trying to give you an understanding of the connection between grace and sin. Picturing it you first get the word (gratos) meaning the center or winning point, usually the center red dot. Miss the mark and you get (sinotos) anything outside the red center being negative point. Without Christ, we will always hit negative points missing the grace point, but with Christ and his grace, we will always hit the grace point.

As the Archer practices to become a discipline shooter of the bow and arrow, we must discipline ourselves in the Word to become children of grace. Jesus Christ taught us these discipline if we only try to discipline if we only try to discover His Word. All we need is there we have to accept it as an undeniable fact. When we are in recovery this might be hard to grasp onto, but God does accept us! The Devil knows this and will try anything unravel you and tear you down. Do not let him get the best of you, stand up and fight! For he is a liar and a thief and we our Children of God, receive God's grace letting it teach you means to live a discipline life. In Psychiatry, we are told that our problems are due to the mistakes of our parents. That might be true, but it is up to us to accept and forgive making the change to recover.

"What are we to do, adrift in a sea of arrogance? Some are nihilistic and say, "Nothing." They purpose that we continue could possibly be charted a vast sea which bring us to any true clarity or meaningful destination. But others, sufficiently aware know that they are lost, dare to hope that they can work themselves out of ignorant through developing even greater awareness." (Peck, The Road Less Traveled, 1979, p. 185) As Dr. M. Peck, states we can come from ignorance too true spiritual health and it just takes a little disappointed, hope, and faith in God or according to what He can do for us. To live in grace and discipline we must become a purposeful person. We must be willing to help those like us (who struggle with mental illness). For those who help others help themselves. Be a person of self-discipline and received a grace from the giver of grace. Stand up and smile saying, I am somebody, because I know my God delights in me. Even though I fail miserably, He still rejoices over me.

Compared to the norm I have come much further than expected of me and that has made me a better person. I chose to write this book for you that reader. It is my greatest pleasure to share with you my life and all the things I learned. I know for fact if we comprehend the discipline of grace we will grow mentally as well as spiritually. Things may seem tough, but if we take them head on, we will learn a great deal about ourselves. So many of us quit when things get a little tough, but there is no need to "throw in the towel". This world may be a lonely place at times it might seem hopeless, but know we have a God that loves us. Know one thing that God's, a disciplinary father who well allow us to reap the consequences of our sin, but He will always give us that the grace to handle the consequences of those inequities.

Dear Lord I fail miserably all the time and do not deserve your kindness. Break my heart weary needs to be mended. Refresh me with your well of living water. Help me dear Lord to receive from you and from others, so in return I can reach out a loving hand. Show me my God I can be a purposeful person dedicated to the response of truth. Teaching to be the best archer, so I may never missed the mark. Show me how to rise up against the adversary who lurks as a roaring lion ready to devour his prey. I want to give you everything instead of just going through the motions. I pray this in your Glorious name that is above all names, receives Glory and honor.

Chapter X

Two Sides
of
a Coin

Have you ever heard it said there are two sides of a coin? Well that goes the same for our emotions. We have the positive side and the negative side. The old saying goes that is their tails you win or lose and for the art of knowing man's emotions, there is positive and negative. We do not have to live with negative emotions, because true feelings are that based on the things around us. If we surround ourselves with negative people, we will become negative. If Surround ourselves with positive people, we will become positive. Can you see what I am getting at here? It is a matter of to do and not to do! Generally, we think that we are doing what is best for us, but contrary to the truth is we are harming what we were intended to be!

Negative emotions start when our emotions have been traumatized by the negative event in the past. It might be an event where we were made to feel like an ant in the dirt. Such things make our self-esteem lower than it has to be or should be. Looking at our emotions from a spiritual aspect, we do not have to feel we need to hide away from the world. Satan plagues our minds with native thoughts dragging us that a spiral emotional roller coaster. We do not have to feel hopeless and abandoned. I know it is hard, because I have been there. It is just a choice I ask you to walk in this *path of recovery*. From time to time, I get plagued with some negative thoughts, but I have learned to rebuke them in Jesus name. No need to whine about it, no one ever said that recovery was going to be easy. "Most of us do not fully see the truth that life is difficult. Indeed a moon more or less incessantly, noisy, or subtly about the abnormity of their problems, burdens and difficulties as if life was generally easy as if life should be easy." (Peck, The Road Less Traveled, 1979, p. 15) Did not Jesus say who ever follows me will be persecuted for my namesake. If we stand out and say I have a mental illness the world will scoff costs us. Recovery takes fortitude and the willingness to do what it takes to become a person of purpose. Correct me if I am wrong, but life does not always come late a basic set of instructions. It would be so much easier if it did, but if you think about it is not that what the bible as! Try reading it you might just be surprised.

Positive thinking comes in a word from God, a kind of gesture from a friend or a song that touches the strings of your heart. How do we who suffer find positive emotions? Simply by searching the heart of

Jesus Christ and our own heart as well. When answers are not enough, there is Jesus! I find it helpful to meditate on the fact that Jesus gave his life on a cross for me. It is helpful to know that Jesus said he wants to lighten our burdens. **Mattew11:28-30** "Come to me, all you who are weary and burdened, and I will give you rest. Take my yoke upon you and learn from me, for I am gentle and humble in heart, and you will find rest for your souls. For my yoke is easy and my burden is light." This is an encouraging thought to think Jesus Christ who died and took everything upon a cross for me would ever want to share my burdens. All I can say is Wow! If you read the Psalms, you will find that even King David lamented when he was feeling down and depressed. In the Psalms, you will discover that its author King David was one of the most troubled individuals in the Bible!

Sometimes when you are feeling a little blue, it is a good thing to read the Beatitudes in the Bible. This is one of Jesus' most beloved and memorable sermons. **Matthew 5:3-12** "Blessed are the poor in spirit, for theirs is the kingdom of heaven. Blessed are those who mourn, for they will be comforted. Blessed are the meek, for they will inherit the earth. Blessed are those who hunger and thirst for righteousness, for they will be filled. Blessed are the merciful, for they will be shown mercy. Blessed are the pure in heart, for they will see God. Blessed are the peacemakers, for they will be called sons of God. Blessed are those who are persecuted because of righteousness, for theirs is the kingdom of heaven. "Blessed are you when people insult you, persecute you and falsely say all kinds of evil against you because of me. Rejoice and be glad, because great is your reward in heaven, for in the same way they persecuted the prophets who were before you." Jesus in these preceding verses gives some awesome promises for reasons to turn the negatives into positives. In moments of helplessness meditate on these verses of scripture you will be a better person for it.

Even in the moments of a darkest time of depression, God still takes delight in us and finds us a pleasure in His eyes. He only asks us to cry out to and ask for His help. Imagine if you can (Satan) before God accusing us for our depression and God boast that even in our depression we will still love Him. We have no need to be depressed all the time, because we can always tap into the fountain of life that flows, an endless supply of living water. Peace comes when we accept our flaws and find ways to use them in creative ways. Please give it a try you will become a person full of purpose. You have nothing to lose when you take the good with the bad. Weigh out the bad and good taking only what can nurture you. Balance is the key to recovery and finding the balance will help you to grow as a person. Making your life flexible can only cause nurturing growth that can only make you better.

Believe me I know that it is hard work! I know that in my daily struggles having the extraordinary flexibility to help others before myself brings joy in knowing I personally helped someone in their recovery to begin to recover. "Balancing is the discipline that gives us flexibility. Extraordinary flexibility is required for successful living in all spheres of life." (Peck, The Road Less Traveled, 1979, p. 64) Doing this has helped me immensely and I am sure it will help you the same way it helped me. What I am asking you to do takes a great amount of effort on your part, but will not regret this major step you about to embark on. The Bible says plainly that true inner peace comes in helping others before you help yourself. Psychiatry might argue against the role of the eternal spirit, but rather they choose to deny it or believe it the evidence is all around us. We find our support in the renewing of our spirit by the inner working of Jesus Christ who gives us strength through the Holy Spirit.

Ephesians 3:14 "For this reason I kneel before the Father, from whom his whole family in heaven and on earth derives its name. I pray that out of his glorious riches he may strengthen you with power through his Spirit in your inner being, so that Christ may dwell in your hearts through faith. I pray that you, being rooted and established in love, may have power, together with all the saints, to grasp how wide and long, high, and deep is the love of Christ to know the love that surpasses knowledge that you may be filled to the measure of all the fullness of God. Now to him who is able to do immeasurably more than all we ask or imagine, according to his power that is at work within us, to him be glory in the church and in Christ Jesus throughout all generations, forever and ever! Amen." Take this prayer and personalize it between you and the Lord putting you and me where necessary. Power is mentioned three times here in different wording and context, so it must be important. (1) Power of the Inner Spirit: As we accept Christ, we receive power that becomes our means to pray with authority. This gives us the ability to love people the way God loves through His Son Jesus Christ. (2) The Power of Knowledge: That is the knowledge of God! We have all the knowledge of God at our fingertips and it is found in the Bible. This knowledge can be our teacher in our *pilgrimage toward recovery*. (3) Workable Power: This is what gives us the ability to move forward and take on challenges. This gives us the means to walk with a sense of purpose and helps us to discover our self-worth.

The Bible is a key tool to our *pilgrimage toward recovery* and I will stress this respectively throughout this book. The Bible is not only a sword or tool it is our main source of nourishment each one of us in our personal recovery to find our spiritual health and wellbeing. You do not have to hide away from the world, step out in faith the world is waiting to benefit from your experience. Be the most diligence, in your faith supplying moral excellence. Galatians 5:22-25 "But the fruit of the Spirit is love, joy, peace, patience, kindness, goodness, faithfulness, gentleness and self-control. Against such things, there is no law. Those who belong to Christ Jesus have crucified the sinful nature with its passions and desires. Since we live by the Spirit, let us keep in step with the Spirit." While in a *pilgrimage toward recovery*, these qualities are yours and they do not render anything useless. Much of these qualities bring-forth fruitfulness that gains respective knowledge of Jesus Christ.

It is long strenuous process to be in recovery, but recovery must take place in our lives. A diligent person who strives for the Fruits of the Spirit begins to develop moral excellence and genuinely succeeds! I use to have poor self-control, but with God's helping hand I have become confident and self-controlled. Success is not measured by how much we do, but more or less, in how well we perform in God's eyes based on our personal moral conduct. I must admit from time to time I still lose my temper, but I am learning to keep my temper in check by trying to find proper boundaries. I learned not to get mad at myself when I cannot do something, because I remind myself there are plenty of things that I can do that make up the difference. Negative thinking only builds up wrong ideas. You have to bring your anger before God and leave it there! What these negative bouts of anger bring out about our-selves is simply not true, so do not believe them.

Sometimes we fail in our *pilgrimage toward recovery* both side of the problem, because we do not want to deal with heartache and pain that comes with it. We hide the pain away, neatly tucked away in our subconscious to become prisoner in our own self-inflicted prison we made. Doing this we put ourselves in a jail of the mind and throw away the key. What might be a common accordance to gain purpose and meaning, only leaves of feeling flat and depressed! "We sometimes feel as if we're in a Heavenly doghouse." (Smith, 2001, p. 57) We do not have to feel this way when God is there to help us though the storms. Read, the Psalms and you will discover most of them written by King David who was in despair 65% of the time. David wrote most of the time laments about the stupid mistakes he made and 35% were David rejoicing over the goodness he saw in God.

God does not turn his ear away from our laments, but rejoices over us! God writes of his rejoicing in His Holy Word! God loves us and wants us to succeed and become a purposeful person. **Zephaniah 3:9** "Then will I purify the lips of the peoples, that all of them may call on the name of the LORD and serve him shoulder to shoulder?" In the simplest of terms, the answer to this question could be the defining moment in our recovery. **Zephaniah 3:17** "The LORD your God is with you, he is mighty to save. He will take great delight in you, he will quiet you with his love, he will rejoice over you with singing." If the God who created the Heavens, the Earth and Humanity who lives on the Earth delights in His creation, how much more should we delight in ourselves. The very fact that God believes in us this way should mean that flipping the coin would be as easy as praying for God to give us a chance.

We do not have to worry that it comes out on tails (negative thinking); because God will make sure, it comes out heads (positive thinking). When you feel stressed out praise God even in mist of your storm and you will get through it. Thank Him for blessing you now and blessings yet to come. Most of all love God and love your-self! Loving ourselves should be ingrained into us as an absolute prime purpose of creating the feeling of love and show tolerance toward fellow *pilgrims in recovery* treating them with the same level of dignity God showed us. Let

God's love generate its warmth inside us and around us and such love will bring an abundance of warmth they will forever change us. If we flip our imaginary coin in mist of the storms trusting in God we will discover that the love of the Son of God is the sole source of light to illuminate our spirit. The brilliancy of Christ light will awaken our spirit to zest and a zeal for life that we never thought we had in us.

It simply starts by flipping the coin and loving ourselves in a manner that creates an emphatic personality that will in part help others. We can all that a soul that is quenched with the love of Christ Jesus it can embark on a positive *pilgrimage toward recovery*. The synergized maturity of the depressed person becoming whole living in the light is beneficial to mental and spiritual health. It is an agreeable point to argue that to love God we must first love ourselves. For spiritual health to grow and flourish becomes crucial to give monetary time in a spirit-diet of the Word of God. A sound mind and sound spirit represents the body as a whole. A healthy amount in God's Word leads to an enriched state of mind and give energy to think positive thoughts. Think and concentrate on what you read and then apply it to your circumstance, thus giving a solution to the problem that you our facing. Flipping the coin then becomes a matter of forgiveness of those who wronged us or wounded us to a degree that we find ourselves trapped in a prison of the mind. Our only reality is the false precepts we base our bias view of self and the act of love. Loving those who love us is easy, but loving those who hurt us is not always easy. To have true recovery we must forgive the past abuser and move on from the pain to become a whole person of sound mind, sound spirit and sound body.

Where we lack to perform an act of love the Holy Spirit can, so let Him do his work in us! First thing, we need to learn is aiming love that is centered and rooted on God. If we seek Him, we will discover that God want to establish an intimate love with us to gain a personal relationship with Him. He longs for us love Him with our heart and soul, so we can receive a love that works at maximum intensity. In the Bible, we are told that God's love is a consuming fire and God want us to turn it back to Him and others. With the inner power of the Holy Spirit, we can show love with same level of intensity that God shows us. The Holy Spirit imparts, to us the personality of God by learning His love toward us not to leave us in the muck and mire. We live in self-centered society and many people have accepted a narcissist life only being concerned with own personal well-being excluding others. In order to recover we need to break away from this narcissist pattern and adapt a more Biblical pattern. It is a sad state of affairs that the world we live has come to revolve in their own personal agendas stepping on others by developing an incapable pattern bonding to no one and loving no one. If we live our life constantly flipping the coin we will never grow.

Dear God help me to begin to think positively. Teach me to put away the negative. Free me from my self-made prison! Create in me a clean heart enriched with praise. Teach me to become a purposeful person so that I can help others. Give me the strength to serve you my God being an example for others to follow. Help me to be a fulfillment of Zephaniah 3:9 and 3:17! I want to serve you my God and be used by you "O" God, so guide me on how to show others to serve and be of service. Keep me Lord thinking positively so that I can be a useful tool to bring Thy glory and honor to a people who struggle from mental illness.

Chapter XI

Via Dela Rosa

Via Dela Rosa comes from the Latin word meaning the road of sorrow. Jesus had to walk is road while carrying a cross that he would be crucifying on dying for all of us. This was referred to in Isaiah as the picture of the suffering servant some 400 years before. **Isaiah 53:1-6** "Who has believed our message and to whom has the arm of the LORD been revealed? He grew up before him like a tender shoot, and like a root out of dry ground. He had no beauty or majesty to attract us to him, nothing in his appearance that we should desire him. He was despised, rejected by men, a man of sorrows, and familiar with suffering; like one from whom men hide their faces he was despised, and we esteemed him not. Surely, he took up our infirmities and carried our sorrows, yet we considered him stricken by God, smitten by him, and afflicted; but he was pierced for our transgressions, he was crushed for our iniquities; the punishment that brought us peace was upon him and by his wounds, we are healed. We all, like sheep, have gone astray, each of us has turned to his own way; and the LORD has laid on him the iniquity of us all." We have no reason to live our life hidden from the world, because Jesus paid the ransom in full. Jesus will certainly be there to walk with us on *pilgrimage toward recovery.*

In Isaiah, we see further persecution that Jesus would have to face, so why can we not see how he is our perfect choice for help? We will read on in Isaiah! Isaiah 53:7-12 "He was oppressed and afflicted, yet he did not open his mouth; he was led like a lamb to the slaughter, and as a sheep before her shearers is silent, so he did not open his mouth. By oppression and judgment, he was taken away. Who can speak of his descendants? For he was cut-off from the land of the living for the transgression of my people he was stricken. He was assigned a grave with the wicked and with the rich in his death, though he had done no violence, nor was any deceit in his mouth. Yet it was the LORD's will to crush him and cause him to suffer, and though the LORD makes his life a guilt offering, he will see his offspring and prolong his days, and the will of the LORD will prosper in his hand. After the suffering of his soul, he will see the light of life and be satisfied; by his knowledge, my righteous servant will justify many, and he will bear their iniquities. Therefore, I will give him a portion among the great, and he will divide the spoils with the strong, because he poured out his life unto death, and was numbered with the transgressors. For he bore the sin of many, and made intercession for the transgressors." Interesting note here is that Jesus who was cut off from his people and paid the ultimate price, his very death on a cross.

Let me ask you then five, why do we still live our life like, we are dead? Get up and seek Jesus that we may live life! Ask him and we will be given a gift that is eternal and that is the grace. If Jesus did all this, why do we still suffer? It is quite simple in order to grow we must learn what it is you suffer. Kahlil Gibran said that in order to know joy one must be familiar with suffering. To live the way we do is nothing short of foolishness, because after seeing the magnificence of our Lord and Savior Jesus Christ we should be filled with joy. Think about it if Jesus Christ can do all this then certainly he can help us to overcome our depression. Jesus knows anxiety and depression, for in the Garden of Gethsemane it said he cried drops of blood. **1Peter 5:7** "Cast all your anxiety on him, because he cares for you. Take the plunge and walk through your suffering to learn what it means to recover. Such lessons than I could teach you would not be as important as that suffering brings forth knowledge and this knowledge gives us wisdom that surpasses even our understanding. Let us, reflect for a moment and think hard about predicament that we got ourselves in, because it is only temporary and there is a light at the end of the tunnel.

God comforts us in our moments of depression no matter how down we really feel. If you can picture a shepherd tending his flock of sheep and as one is young, he gathers him up in his arms and carries to a place of rest and safety. **Isaiah 40:11** "He tends his flock like a shepherd: He gathers the lambs in his arms and carries them close to his heart; he gently leads those that have young." Here God is the shepherd and it shows me that those of us who are young, inexperienced and depressed He will comfort us nurturing us to a place of rest and solitude. Sometimes our disabilities seem a little overwhelming, but in Christ, we have many options to use to help us gain ground on our sanity. "God himself is to be delighted in not simply for what he does and he gives, but for whom he is. They shepherd King speaks of a vital relationship between our delight and the desires of our hearts. What a magnificent invitation!" (Smith, 2001, p. 28) As Scotty Smith so elegantly shows that contrast between God's nature and his delight in his creation (humanity) we are shown a glimpse of divine love.

If we can never be perfect, why do we fight God's plan for our lives at every turn? In simple, terms we are in all aspects creatures of habit and it is our habitual nature that when things get overwhelming to go into hibernation. Even though as creatures of habit, as humans we can learn to overcome these habitual habits. Let us look at Jesus as an example as we discover our mental illness for what it is then that is an anguished or torment, we cannot control of our own free will. For argument sake, some would say that if he was God and he could not have suffered in the way he did. Remember it all Jesus was also in all aspects fully human as much as he was fully God. Remember I said earlier in the book that Jesus faced anxiety at Gethsemane crying tears of blood well he had to face similar feeling and the cross. By taking on the sins of the world, God would have to turn his head away from his Son Jesus Christ. For Jesus cried out on the cross Eloi, Eloi Lama Sabachni (Father, Father, Why have you Forsaken me) feeling the loss of the father he knew from eternity past.

Every cry that Jesus cried upon the cross he cried in anguish and pain like no one could ever experience. Jesus suffered extreme separation anxiety from his separation from his Eternal Father. When dealing so depressed that we cannot stand think about how Jesus must have felt in how she can truly understand us. "If you think you are not then you are beaten you are. If you think you dare not, you do not! If you want to win but think you cannot it is almost a cinch you will not. If you think you will lose you have lost it." (Anderson, 1990-2000, p. 114) We could even go as far to say that he had a sense of fearful anxiety, because he was to face the torment of Hell and death. It would be an understatement to say after reading all this that Jesus could not be an example of how to overcome and recover from our depression. Believe me I can say from personal the theological study that I can say Jesus as has been there!

When we are weak minded and fragile imprisoned in our mind we should not act as cowering prisoners full of self-doubt. There is no need to become prisoners in such a manner as this, this will only lead us to be more depressed. **Isaiah 51:14** "The cowering prisoners will soon be set free; they will not die in their dungeon, nor will they lack bread. For I am the LORD your God, who churns up the sea so that its waves roar—the LORD Almighty is his name." The bread is the bread of life (God's Word). God will protect you and free you from your fears and self-doubt. Believe me I have walked down my own Via Dela Rosa! Been born with Cerebral Palsy, A.D.D., Anxiety and LDS (Learning Disability Syndrome) having many obstacles in my life overcome. Yes, I had many challenges in my *pilgrimage toward recovery*, but I chose to become a fighter and to overcome becoming a better person.

The first Jesus Christ for the first time at first it seemed unlivable way to live, but the more I knew him the easier it became. I know at times and it feels hopeless, but we have so much too late for, that my fellow pilgrims this is where God is showing us the bigger picture. "Virtually everything we participate in teaches and affirms that you get what you earn and you are what you do and have." This can most definitely be applied as well as help us to grow and come out of our depression. I never had a day where I was not depressed, but in the hardship, I learned a valuable lesson in that is to find discipline in grace! It is true we all face anxiety differently and stress in different ways. Why do we not seek help from our peers? A community of peers if you let it can come in handy when you need a friend to talk too. Why live a sheltered and fearful life of what others think about you? If you come up with a negative response to this question, than you need to reevaluate yourself and find the solution. I know it is a struggle to reach out when you are broken inside, but the Bible reminds us that we have an eternal path that leads us to peace and rest. **1Peter 5:7** "I write these things your children who believe that you may have eaten alive." They should be your confirmation of victory! He did not say guests, hope or even pray, but know we have eternal life!

Go ahead, you have nothing to lose just ask God and he will commit himself to helping you and your recovery. It seems at times we are too comfortable in our own Via Dela Rosa to let him in. Commit yourself too self-evaluation and allow God to work in you and through you. For this, I am afraid you will have to come out of the shadows in the darkness they cast and be willing to be exposed. At times, it is hard to go out into any community when it feels like everyone is tearing at you. I have those moments to, but it those times I have to force myself to be among people. Satan wants us to think people are really seeing us, to prevent us from letting us see ourselves as God sees us. Is only prevents people from seeing what God has done for us. **Psalm 40:1-4** "I waited patiently before the lord and He heard my cry. He took me out of the mud and mire; He set my feet upon a rock and gave me a firm place to stand. He has put a new song in my mouth a hymn of praise onto our God. Many will see and hear putting their trust in the Lord." So do as they say is and put our entire trust in the Lord!

I know that you know the difference between a lie and a promise, so why do you or Heaven's sake sit on your pity-pot? Why do you wallow in self-doubt? "I was brought face to face with my own misplaced trust and love. Seeing that I trusted in things more than I trusted God hurt. Realizing that I love things more than I loved Jesus hurt even more. Accepting that I was powerless to change myself brought a strange modicum of hope. Though overwhelmed, I sense I was being swallowed alive by an enormous providence—kind of like the finish swallowed Jonah." (Smith, 2001, p. 91) By letting these things in a way of God, we are putting our trust in the circumstances that impale us. We should trust in God and God alone! There comes a time we have to let go and let God, I am still learning this one! Asked my wife and she will tell you that I still stumble on this very thing.

At this point in the *pilgrimage for recovery*, we must put our entire hope and trust in the God who created us. I must admit I can still stumble upon this very thing repeatedly, because sometimes I guess it is just human nature rearing its ugly head. When circumstances arise I seem to fall apart, but God is teaching me to trust him in all things. It is hard to see at times that God is in control, but there is no circumstance that God cannot deal with and show us through. Jesus took being beaten, mocked, spit at and nailed to a cross to show us how much he really love us. Then he arose from the grave and conquered death and giving us hopeless sinner's new life. It Jesus did all that then he surely can help us in our darkest hour of depression and anxiety. Believe me I cried out on my knees many times in the answer to my anxiety. Sometimes I find myself caught up in the status quo being used for futile logic. Then I am brought down to size and humble the only way God can!

Sometimes a condition gets us so overwhelmed we forget who God is and what He can do for us. The devil always tries to remind us of our past mistakes when we are trying to recover and he will try anything and everything in his limited power to keep us down. His only means of discouraging us is whispering negative thoughts in our mind to keep us in the suffering mode. Do not let him do this, for we are better than that. We are children of God in Christ, so start acting like children of God! Simply tell the devil to back off and step aside, for I am on a *pilgrimage toward recovery*. Nothing you can do or ever feel that can make God stop loving you. He went as far as sending His Son to die on across, what more do you need to give it all to Him and just simply believe. We give our problems to Him and our disbelief take them back putting the blame on Him, when the blame really belongs to us. Just bring your fears, self-doubts, depression and anxiety to the foot of the cross and leave them there. Then turn and walk away not looking back no matter what the advisory tells you.

"Sometimes it is easier not to hope, especially if you are terrified of the possibility of pain." (Smith, 2001, p. 111) Then God calls us into the harsh reality of the discipline of grace. It is here that we truly discover who we are and who we will become. This is a time for self-discovery accepting and asking for nothing but our own sanity. On the very cross, that Christ suffered and died becomes our very place of refuge. Daily I walked each an everyday my own Via Dela Rosa, doing it with a sense of purpose that I discovered in accepting Jesus Christ. This has been my solitude and my renewed purpose for a more abundant life

Dear God I walk down my own Via Dela Rosa and lay them down at the foot of the cross. I cry out my laments through suffering! I lay down all my depression, self-doubt, anxiety, frustration and fears. Help me to have strength to walk away. Send me an angel like you sent for your Son Jesus Christ. Lift me up when I drowning in my fears and show me how to live for you Lord Jesus Christ. Break my heart and restore me do away with my selfish pride. Guide me on the path has I learn to handle things. Let me let you do what you need to through me. You own my life so help me to trust you more.

Amen

Chapter XII

Refuge in Love

The love of God is our resting place and refuge from the storms of life. I find this to be true when I am under attack from negative thoughts. The love of God is greater than our problems, so why live in disappear when we have our hope in God! Sometimes our fears get to overwhelming and they overcome our mind and spirit. The love of God can and will lift us out of depression. "What would it feel like in our heart to know God not only accepts you, but that He richly rejoices over us you?" For me it was an awesome revelation to discover that God loves and rejoices over me. (Smith, 2001, p. 26) **Zephaniah 3:16-17** "On that day they will say to Jerusalem, "Do not fear, O Zion; do not let your hands hang limp. The LORD your God is with you, he is mighty to save. He will take great delight in you, he will quiet you with his love, he will rejoice over you with singing." Take this to heart and you might find the truth and that is that God loves beyond what you can fathom. If God love you in such a manner as this, why accept a life of depression? Rejoice in your weakness, God does!

I find refuge in the common fact that God helps me to fly like an eagle in the mist of storms. It is awesome to know that while depressed God is there to comfort us and lift the negative thoughts that plague my mind. It was hard for me to accept that God loves me and would quiet my soul and take my problems away. **Isaiah 30:18** "Yet the LORD longs to be gracious to you; he rises to show you compassion. For the LORD is a God of justice. Blessed are all who wait for him!" When I discovered the love that God had for me it was like turning on a light switch understanding for the first time my true potential and the intentions that God had for a purposeful person. It was like a spark that lit my spirit giving me a renewed hope for recovery. Discovery of this is the key to our recovery and the means that might just help us change. Correct what needs to be corrected giving it all over to the one who wants to heal you. God is waiting to bless you and heal you, so just reach out and take His hand. In those moments of depression call out to God and praise Him, you will feel a whole lot better.

I know that from my own experience that it seems there is no rest or hope for us. The torments in our minds will not let us rest and it seems no one truly understands that they just pretend to care. For it is when we take refuge in Christ Jesus that we can find true hope and rest. Jesus understands the fact that rest is hard to find. **Mattew8:20** "Jesus replied, "Foxes have holes and birds of the air have nests, but the Son of Man has no place to lay his head." Reading this scripture, shows me that Christ understood about not have rest. If God sent His son to die for you, how much more would He love you? Jesus loved us so much that He gave up His life you. He rose from the dead and conquered death so that we might have life.

To grasp how God loves you must first know who God is and to know who He is we must understand His personality. John tells that God is love and love is God. If love, He is than love is His personality! **1Corinthians 13:4-8** "God is patient, God is kind, God does not envy, God does not boast, God is not proud. God is not rude, God is not self-seeking, God is not easily angered, God, keeps no record of wrongs. God love does not delight in evil but rejoices with the truth. God always protects, always trusts, always hopes, and always perseveres. God never fails. (Emphasis is mine)! This verse is commonly known as the love chapter, but the point I was trying to make is that if love is God than the love chapter would be his personality. God is love He is the author and finisher of all wisdom. When God gave His only son to die for us, we were able to view a peace that surpasses all understanding. **Philippians 4:7** "And the peace of God, which transcends all understanding, will guard your hearts and your minds in Christ Jesus." This very peace is our strength, not to be anxious about anything! **Philippians 4:6** "Do not be anxious about anything, but in everything, by prayer and petition, with thanksgiving, present your requests to God." These verses have been a big help to me in my recovery, because when I get anxious I just remember these verses and my anxiety subsides.

When we think of the refuge of love, we think of comfort or the sense of being safe at home. "The same love, delight, and pleasure God the Father has for God the Son He has for those who are in Christ no exceptions." (Smith, 2001, p. 37) Like and eagle watches over and protects her young her young God watches over and protects us. An eagle would die to protect her young God sent His only Son to die for us. Saying that we take refuge in love literally means to be kept safe from eternal death. When we accept Christ, we have the gift of the Holy

Spirit, which in Greek is paraklētos means comforter and teacher. When we have the means to be comforted, so why not tap into the source.

Refuge comes when we began to understand God's Word and learn to pray the word more effectively. As you read the God's Word, meditate on the particular verses that you read. In doing this, God's Word comes alive as if it comes right off the page. "For the Christian, to be spiritually alive is to being union with God by being in Christ. That is the way Greek word zoë is used in the New Testament. In fact, being in Christ Jesus the theme of the New Testament. Adams sinned and his union with god ours as well was severed. It is God's external plan to bring human creation that to Him-self and restore the union. He enjoyed union with Adam at creation. That restored with God, which we find in Christ, is the essence of our identity." (Anderson, 1990-2000, p. 26) I have tried in my past relationships to have compatibility, but they all failed due to my mental incompatibility issues. These cause many failed relationships and many disappointments in my life. Do not get me wrong, I have learned from all these misfortunes and have become a stronger person.

Now I have found someone compatible to me and in one sense, I have become a teacher and she a student, likewise I have become a student and she has become my teacher. Where she is most weak I am strong and where I am week she is strong. Both of us have our own inconsistencies, but we seem to complement each other. Becoming alive to each other was not easy, but we have put Christ Jesus in the center of our relationship. This has been an interesting and yet very different thing to me, because I have found someone who truly understands me! I find my refuge and hope in her smile in the way she looks at me with any Christ like love. For people like you and me to be in a loving relationship is a great task, but in Christ the can be made smooth. I have learned much about myself from being married. My wife and I have our arguments, but how we handle the arguments that make a difference in our relationship. Praying for wisdom and grace to forgive is the key no matter what is said to the other person.

In the reality of things, what keeps me going is to have the assurance can know that Jesus Christ did not die for nothing! When you get depress meditate on the fact that Jesus Christ died so that we will do not deserve it would have the eternal life. Look inside yourself and you might find the truth, which is the fact that you have a purpose. How can a depressed person, such as our-selves have a purpose? When you come to grips with your own mental inconsistencies you will find that true meaning and purpose is found in and the hope of relying on Jesus Christ. Find hope in discovering that in helping others we begin to grow on our way to becoming a purposeful person in a *pilgrimage toward recovery*. In grasping the very essence of love, we soon discover that it is the heart of the child's faith that we can move the very mountains of despair. Nothing is impossible with God, so why would we want to continue in despair? I know from experience that in these hard to take that first step into unfamiliar territory of discovering our inner-self. Stepping out of our comfort zone is the only way we will find true recovery.

To love and be loved is the hardest thing anyone would ask you to do, but this has to be done. You are a child of God and you have a purpose, so find out what purpose God has bore you and clinch it. "Difficult circumstances and hard provinces often become a means by which the Holy Spirit quickens I were thirst for the fountain of life that God alone opens up. No one and nothing can satisfy the cravings he has placed in the hearts of his children. We are most sane and three when we live in the light of this truth." (Smith, 2001, p. 86) Let God take the reins letting him work in you and through you. Picture this! God is the potter and we are the clay, so allow him to continue to create in us his perfect creation. Find meaning in perplexity and the rise to the occasion and begin to recover. Our recovery comes as we grow and discover who we are in Christ and what our purpose is in Christ.

In our craving to recover, God has given us the means we just need put it into action. For if we learned how to pray and meditate upon prayer, we find our purpose. Why lie in a feeling of waste, when there is so much more life can offer? You always hear this common saying "life sucks and then you die" and people go through life feeling this way. Do not fall into that trap of Satan trying to make you feel that you are better off dead. In Christ, we are made to come alive! So do not live life this way. Step out in the faith and learn the power of loving others! Refuse comes in self-discovery in finding Christ in the mist of the pain and taking that final step to reach out to the only one who cares. We will find that in our *pilgrimage toward recovery* that helped comes in the most unlikely places and unlikely people. This is where we must learn to humble our-selves and take the help that is offered.

God is your only refuge in wake of your depression, so give up yourself entirely to God and let him become your safe haven. Reflect on the awesomeness of God! Let yourself show as the very art or handiwork of God. God will bless you if you only call out to him. (**Psalm 2:12**) "Blessed are those who take refuge in him." Take that chance and go to the bare resource of your recovery and that is the love of God our Creator and you will find a hand stretched out to comfort you.

Many people believe that mental illness stem from chemical deficiency in the brain. Western Psychiatric medicine has helped to make our bodies adapt to low and high doses Psychiatric medicine, but the symptoms usually last a lifetime. Psychiatric systems must be something else besides chemical, do not you agree? Chemical difficulties are caused by several factors that can combine together to make matters worse. Coming to (Point A), we learn courage is a vital virtue in our *pilgrimage toward recovery*, because courage establishes a clear point in which to explore new horizons in recovery sand the strength come from God's grace working in us. Taking the step forward into recovery we begin to execute the wisdom needed to triumph over frustration and rise above our per sieved limitations we put on ourselves giving us a fresh perspective on the life God wants us to walk in our *pilgrimage toward recovery*. Learn to go beyond Point A and become better equipped to understand the purpose and direction we need not to become afraid to move forward. Take a leap of faith and discover how to move forward with a heightened sense of self-worth and self-confidence essential to our goals.

Lord, I am broken and naked before my peers as hands reach out to harm me. Help me to take refuge in your helping and strong arms. I find myself in an uncaring world not willing to help. Give me strength to face the day for I am weak and lost. I do not know why and many more and I need you to come and rescue me. Dear Lord I need you to help me to walk in your light! I want to serve you, but my depressed state of mind will not let me be. Dear God I fall on my face before you seeking your presence to find that grace backing change in the Anne rearrange these broke in Soul. I plead with you God in the creating me to find peace and rest in this forest blackened by the trees in the shadows they cast over my life.

Amen

Chapter XIII

Starting From Point A

Point A is a recovery point of reference and light of the wisdom needed to find recovery. Before I go into depth about this particular type of wisdom, let me give you an overview of my life. I was born with Scoliosis a form of Cerebral Palsy having crooked knees in the spine shaped liked a shoehorn. The Scoliosis Cerebral Palsy has gotten the best of me, because the lower part of my spine has chipped away and I have sharp pains that shoot up and down my spine then in my arms legs and knees. Also, cause of complications to the brain that arose when I was born I was left with LDS (Learning Disability Syndrome) staying back two years in the second grade. Much of school was very difficult, but I got into regular classes by 10th grade and graduated at age 20 and 1985. I became a Christian in the summer of 85 and began to read not only the Word of God and every book I could get my hands on. I traveled from Massachusetts to Vermont, back to Massachusetts in northern Greenfield. Then back to Vermont and in March 1985 I moved down to Franklin Tennessee and stayed there for about 10 years.

In March of 2003, I moved East Hartford Connecticut where I finally had an IQ tests and I learned that my IQ fell in the 75% and 85 percentile being about average. The Psychologist who did the test said that even though my IQ might have been low I had so much stored in my long-term memory that it was hard to get an accurate reading possibly making me smarter than most would think me to be. I also discovered I had A.D. D. (Attention Deficit Disorder), wow that explain a lot. I was put on Sraterra and I discovered that I really could concentrate and I wished I had discovered the sooner, but I believe everything happens for a reason and I possibly needed to struggle a little and learn so that I would be where I am now. I also have Depression, Anxiety & Panic Attacks and Insomnia. These may to some seem like limitations that might make my *pilgrimage toward recovery* a hard struggle, but it is my determination and power infused by the Holy Spirit that would never let me give up. In light of these physical and mental limitations, I am nothing short of a walking miracle. I am a published poet and sitting here writing a book about my life is quite an accomplishment. For someone like me who might have been written off as retarded, I have made some considerable and amazing accomplishments.

I am still asked that question, why has not God healed you? My answer is that God does not create junk! I would not want him to change a thing, because I know he can use me just as I am to help those who struggle like me. If I was healed and make perfect in mind and body, would I still want help those who struggle through life! Probably not, I would lose the sense of understanding that I have for those who suffer in a world that tries to be perfect. I believe God uses that broke in and the frail to be in an effective tool to show his glory showing through our weakness his strength. If the world could see a broken person in mind, body and spirit becoming more and he was thought that he could ever be, how much more of a witness would he be? I know this, because I have been down and out for so long that I had to do something. I just had to come up fighting, fighting for my recovery and to stand my ground and boldly say I am somebody.

I stand here only because the Grace of God has given me the stability to begin to recover. Oddly, my wisdom stems from growing up with an alcoholic father who most of the time made f fun of me. When I graduated high school in June of 1985, I heard him yelling at my mother, I wish I never had the retard for a son. Now most people with let this become so depressed they would be unable to cope, but me it just fueled the fire within me to succeed no matter how harsh the criticism would be. God was not going make it easy, for I would have to go through many test and temptations.

When I was in the 12th grade, I started drinking like a fish and this would last for about 21 years. I would go to church and on the weekends, I would consume what most people would drink in a week I would consume in one day. This was one in my heart is battles to overcome, but constantly being on my knees finally we gave it all to God he took it all away in 2006 and I have a drunken sense. During this battle or war that raged on with its ups & downs, I read such authors and as Carl Jung, Dr. M. Scott Peck, Dr. Neil Anderson, Max Luccado, Kahlil Gibran and many others. My knowledge became prudent, pungent and fulfilling. It was Kahlil Gibran who said, you that you gain wisdom one must become familiar with sorrow and a friend to pain. For it is in our moments of the darkest sufferings that we discovered the wisdom to recover. As we suffer, we learn about ourselves what we are made of. In essence, suffering should be our familiar foe as familiar as a Family Friend.

This may seem harsh, but do this and I promise that you will become a purposeful person. In times of suffering, we find God and discover how he is the Author of Wisdom! **Psalm 111:10** "The fear of the LORD is the beginning of wisdom; all who follow his precepts have good understanding. To him belongs eternal praise." **Proverbs 2:6** For the LORD gives wisdom, and from his mouth come knowledge and understanding. In your moments of grief meditate on these verses and you will gain much-needed insight in your *pilgrimage toward recovery*. Never get too proud of your accomplishments and be humble and everything you learn in your recovery. When approached in a negative way, never act like the world in lash out with a harsh word. **Proverbs 11:12** "A man who lacks judgment derides his neighbor, but a man of understanding holds his tongue." In doing this you will be well underway to recovery and will discover that, you have more fortitude and you ever realize. Good company brings health and prosperity.

You remember when we talk about the discipline and grace that had true humility! Will understand is one thing, it is in grace and discipline are humbled by wisdom by those who are wise. In the same aspect of all rational thought, we face hardship when we trust in foolishness and those who antiquates the ways of foolish folly. **Proverbs 13:20** "Those who walk with a wise grows wise, but those who are companion to fools suffer much harm." I love this verse and is one that I live by. It is still true that we find comfort by the company we keep, when we seem to get the depressed and pull ourselves down think about the company that we have kept in those times. **Proverbs 14:3** "He who guards his lips guards his life, but he who speaks rashly will come to ruin." Think about this and buy it and he will soon discover that you have inner wisdom. For in this I can say, watch what you say and she will grow into a person of understanding. Do not let the foolish things of this world ever make you feel depressed, for you are a much better person than that. You will soon discover that!

As we get older, we begin to discover our own coping mechanisms. We find prudence and through this, we gain a better sense of self-worth. Here you will become a simpleminded man of prudence who in the light of wisdom guides his steps. In trying to be prudent, do not become so simpleminded that the lack sound judgment, but think prudently giving thought to every step. It is in such wisdom that we discover the necessariness for why we suffer. It in living a life of prudence that we rediscover the path we need to walk in the recovery process. "How can we reconcile the claim that we are the objects of God's affection, with the reality of human suffering?" (Smith, 2001, p. 145) The answer to this can be found in the craftiness of genuine love. We discover this in our willingness to open ourselves up to the Creator and Lover of our Souls. If God loved us enough to send His only Son to die for us, do you really think He would leave in the pit of depression? Only a fool would not come to a God who loves them the God does, but we do it every day when we lay around depressed. Love is an action not just a feeling!

Love is an allusive state of mind that calls for action to step out in faith and show love! Notice how love is crafty and decisive in her ways and you will find peace in mist of the storms of life. Love used in the wrong way can wound a person deeply, but love used the right way can heal a person. Being called to be lovers of God we are asked to love others better than we love ourselves. That means that we love people's faults and not just their strengths. For when you genuine love you begin to recover from your depressed state of mind. You cannot be wise and you cannot recover if you hide from the pain your entire life. **Proverbs 19:11** "A man's wisdom gives him patience; it is to his glory to overlook an offense." Thus, we learn what it means to love yourself heart, mind, body & spirit and I assure you that you find the grace to help you to continue in the process of recovery. In light of this, your eyes will be opened to whole, new way of living and you will not want to go back to being depressed. When you take a stance as a prudent person, you will develop a set of values that will sustain you in those depressed moments in time.

Coming back around and start from point A we need to be prudent and wise knowing that in the essence of all things love come to measure our worth. Our sense of worth is far more important and valuable anything you can buy! For our prudent living in the spirit of love, we soon discover are reason for pain. How can you find love in the mist of pain? God did at His Sons expense, He found us! A prudent also finds success in by focusing on his *pilgrimage toward recovery*. We need to focus on God He has prepared to do. This is a life-changing thing I am asking you to do and it takes loving when it is hard to love. Do not be a fool who waits a lifetime to get help, because you will only fail.

"Focusing on God's goals will lead to ultimate success: Success in God's terms. Peter promises that, as these qualities increase in your life through practice you will be fruitful and will not stumble. That's success!" (Anderson, 1990-2000, p. 145) It is also a prudent person. Take advice from peers and do not fear self-stringent criticism. Take every spoken word and every thought and way it out to see what it can teach you. Be a prudent person who does not try to erase their most invaluable parts of themselves they will comes to grips with it instead.

Seek council in Jesus Christ on how to truly understand anxiety and if he can show a way out of the forest of fear. Given the conditions and circumstance we are in at the time a person can learn how not to become constantly anxious in all degrees of this culture driven by speed performance. Many self-help techniques are not guaranty cure, but can help you cope with the symptoms. For me deep breathing, praying and meditating of the Word of God helps. Going back to point A we need to reach out to a councilor, friend or Pastor for the other mental health issues this brings fourth.

Dear Lord, give to me patience to be a person of purpose prudent in all my decisions. Come into my soul and bathe me from all the crud that bills up. Show me your wisdom. Help me to be wise and make prudent decisions. Help me to pray when I am weak. Give me the patience to help other people like me and lift me up guiding my steps.

Chapter XIV

Canada Dry Kind of Feeling

I know that your thinking the name of soft drink has no place being in a book on mental illness, on the contrary it will make sense as we get further into this chapter. My allegorical look is how the soul gets dry, like when you have that dry feeling in your throat and stomach. When our lives begin to get dry in thought and word we need to cleanse the thirst. In the Bible Jesus said that his Well never runs dry so we need to go to the source to fill our spirit when it runs dry from problems that come up in life. On the last and greatest day of the Feast, Jesus stood and said in a loud voice, (**John 7:37-38**) "If anyone is thirsty, let him come to me and drink. Whoever believes in me, as the Scripture has said, streams of living water will flow from within him." These steams of living water can put life in our spirit that can revive us from being worn out by years of abuse. Life has many challenges and the stream of living water spoken here can be source of strength for better living.

What causes us our spirit to go dry like Canada Dry? It is several things, but the number one reason is strife! In trying to do things on our own we develop a spirit raging with strife giving us nothing but stress. When this happens, we become dry longing to have our spiritual thirst satisfied. (**Proverbs 17:1**) "Better a dry crust with peace and quiet than a house full of feasting, with strife." Our adversary the devil wants strife in our life, because it keeps us from talking to each other and or God. Why do we listen to one who only wants to tear us down and lead us into strife? The answer to this question is to build our self-esteem and to do that we must take what we have learned in the earlier chapters on who we are in God. My fellow pilgrim our self-esteems lies in the arms of Christ, so become a model of Christ and all else will fail in comparison. Is not it better to avoid strife? We should take every effort to avoid strife, but we choose not to listen to wisdom and go the route of suffering. (**Proverbs 20:3**) "It is to a man's honor to avoid strife, but every fool is quick to quarrel." We do not listen to this, but instead drag our feet kicking and screaming while in those dry times in matters of the spirit. We wallow in self-pity complaining not realizing that we had something to do with it in the first place. This, Canada Dry feeling should never get to the point that is overwhelms into getting depressed. We have an endless well of living water (Gods Word) to enrich our lives!

We give the mockers a foot-hole to drain us any sense of value. Give the devil a chance and he will take away everything you thirst for toward God Word. Jesus knew this and that is why he quoted scripture back at the devil to let him know that He stand on the Word of God. The tempter came to him and said, "If you are the Son of God, tell these stones to become bread. **Matthew 4:4** "Jesus answered, "It is written: 'Man does not live on bread alone, but on every word that comes from the mouth of God." Still we choose to live in strife even though God is our source for life, but we do not have to live this life of conflict and self-doubt. The choice is up to you to make the effort toward recovery and if you do not then you will fall into depression. (**Proverbs 22:10**) "Drive out the mocker, and out goes strife; quarrels and insults are ended." Doing this we may learn how to live by the spirit. The life we live is based how we treat others over ourselves. Hate yourself and you hate others. Stir up anger and you will be filled with strife.

The Bible has some strong words to say about strife and anger! In (Proverbs 6) we that God hate's those who spread strife among family. God calls for unity and love those who work toward peace. God made us for unity with one another and unity with Him. The more you understand strife it become clear that God does not think kindly of anyone who instigates strife in the family of God. (**Proverbs 30:30**) "For as churning the milk produces butter, and as twisting the nose produces blood, so stirring up anger produces strife." Strife never accomplishes anything worth putting our efforts into, except that Canada Dry feeling that leaves us wanting more. At this point, we ask God where he is when he is right we left him. God let the winds take us until we turned back and looked for him. God will not continually chase us, so do not keep running. We listen to fools and we will only receive foolishness. Listen to the Wisdom of the Word of God and we will receive peace for our *pilgrimage toward recovery*. Like, the desert runs dry and barren our spirits runs dry from constant strife! No need to put yourself down cause the God who created you breathed life into you so live like you are alive!

While on our *pilgrimage toward* recovery, we need to keep in mind that is an inconvenience to post modern reality. It is never a good time to be crucified or buried even if it is in a spiritual sense. The plus to this comes in the fact that we are baptized in Christ and all past sin is wiped clean. Our hearts must always be opened to the inner working of Christ in our lives. The best time to do the will of God is in the now! Deeper waters flow in the presence of the Lord God and tapping into this deep water draws you closer, never becoming dry in spirit for a long time. I am not saying that you will never go dry, but that when you do you have an enormous source of living water to go too. Hoping for some magical solution to our problems only will leave us disappointed. Walk guided by the Holy Spirit and you will develop a full proof plan of recovery. You will find some degree of mystery to walking in the Holy Spirit that cannot be captured in any equation or formula, but only in Christ himself.

A spirit-filled life-walk is one of true love and true love humility. I wrote about love and humility in the previous chapters, has both play an important part in our walk with God. God does not want us to continue in our dry spells, but we continue to do so. At the times when we doubt the abilities and ourselves, my only advice is to discover how unique God has created us. You will soon discover that you have all the necessary abilities ingrained in you. Rise up and seek God and you will find that you our better equipped than thought. "Some fugitives actually long to be caught; some addicts wants desperately to get busted and Christians, especially Christian leaders, craved to be freed from the disparity between their hearts." (Smith, 2001, p. 18) As Pastor Scotty Smith so eloquently show we all need to be released from our dryness of the mind and spirit. Life is a series of trials and test only to make us stronger. Never self-doubt yourself, but live as a purposeful person full of purpose and desire. God made us to fellowship with Him and until we understand this, we will never be able to be free from depression.

Our craving for peace comes when we are deprived and lacking in grace to get through the depression. Rediscover God for yourself and you will discover that He longs to be close to His creation. God is more than capable of helping us through the depravity of prison of depression. Being depressed in the spirit realm is depriving God. It is like building blinders and walls not letting anyone from coming in including God. We need to discover the strength that God gives us that dwells in us by way of the Holy Spirit. What makes us want to become introverts? I know that for me it was negative remarks said to me by my father. I still have a hard time accepting correction even if it meant as constructive criticism. I battle with negative thoughts every day, but I have discovered better ways of dealing with them. My spirit gets those Canada Dry feelings a lot, but God has become my source of refuge. There are times that I feel like being in a desert without water to drink. I go to God for those times when nothing can quench my spiritual thirst with a living stream of water that will never be quenched.

Pray and the Lord will answer you even when you do not feel He does not. I have found this to be true, but I still at times get overwhelmed by circumstances that go not the way I want them to. In life, it is hard not to let the negative things of life get you get overwhelmed; especially you and me, because we have a legitimate excuse to. Dealing with depression this way only makes us feel worse, so go to the source Jesus Christ! Some day this will come true for all of us who struggle, you only have to believe it. The Canada Dry feeling only leaves us feeling condemned to a life of despair. **Jeriamiah17:16** "I have not run away from being your shepherd; you know I have not desired the day of despair. What passes my lips is open before you." God desires to shepherd us through the times of despair if we only let him try. God does not want us to lack what we need to live, so why not let God take the reins.

"What is that our heart connect better in the fellowship of weakness and hope rather than in the area of competence and performance?" (Smith, 2001, p. 87) The answer simply lies in the fact that we act upon our positional responses; these positional responses become a psychotherapeutic pose deriving from abuse. You and I have the tendency not to show our weakness leaving us with hopelessness deep into our lives. Thus, there goes that Canada Dry feeling making you feel weak and vulnerable. Strive to have the competence not only to do it, but also to believe that it can be done. Dealing with the Canada Dry feeling takes discipline found engaging in diligent execution outperforming the depressed way that we feel. The role should enthusiastic, passionate, ambitious and focusing on quenching the Canada Dry depression. This is where we should manage our time and inspire to criticize, praise, encourage and comfort ourselves. Be an individual struggling to live life not by the false standards of the world, but by God's standards. Such strategies take time an involve trading off short-term goals and recovery strategies. The benefits to this will be the willingness to make choices that inspire others as well as yourself. These choices if we let them can empower us to overcome the Canada Dry feeling and live free of depression. Your anxiety does not have to overtake you, but you can overtake your anxiety!

At times this means practicing what you preach and when it is convenient to do so do what is most important to your recovery. Many people do not believe that people who struggle with Mental Illness can recover and to be strategically, succeeding beyond our limitations. I know that at times we feel under significant and easily pressured by outside forces. At most, we need to rely on striving toward recovery. This calls for us to strategies ways to encourage others building ways to get over the obstacles within our *pilgrimage toward recovery*. I find it hard to find competence in my performance & myself, because I live my life worrying if I failed. Although I still fail at this, Jesus reminds me that He is in control and I need to give Him the reins. In our *pilgrimage toward recovery* we need to seek God to find belief in ourselves and the fact that God can show us on a daily basis to learn more about myself through God's eyes!

Life can make anyone have that Canada Dry feeling and leave us feeling hopeless, but many refuse to admit to it. I still feel dry in my spirit, but if I pray, I force myself to get out of my comfort zone. Prayer is very important and one of the things I have stressed over & over again, because prayer is our plug into the infinite mind of God. Train your brain to eliminate the repetitive negative thinking. It will otherwise lead to dry and ill-responsive thinking, which causes ill-rational reasoning toward depression. When Canada Dry feeling takes over making you feel like throwing in the towel, think on the positive things that you can use to perform better. Make it your goal not to have that dry feeling again, but full of vigor and refreshing life giving water. We are the ones who chose how we are going to live so live it!

Help me dear Lord not to think irresponsibly, but instead to think positively. Give me the strength to see what cannot be seen! Make me a person who seeks you when I have a dry spirit. Make my mind pure and full of wisdom. When it comes to living a pure life I fall short, so purify my soul daily. Give me the holy desire to read your word. Give me spiritual eyes so that your word comes alive to me and dwells in my heart. Teach me 'O' Lord to be an example and teach others the *pilgrimage toward recovery*.

Chapter XV

Extreme Life

An extreme life is a set of rules and regulations that in their use lead us to actual recovery. I am not perfectly recovered by any means the word, but I have found peace. Sometimes in the process of recovery, our medication becomes our god, because if we do not feel immediate effects we think we need more. (**Exodus20:3**) "You shall have no other gods before me." Medication becomes our cutch to lean on when God should be the one lean on we should not fear, for God is our strength in the mist of the storms. (**Isaiah 54:10–12**) "Though the mountains be shaken and the hills be removed, yet my unfailing love for you will not be shaken nor my covenant of peace be removed," says the LORD, who has compassion on you; 'O' afflicted city, lashed by storms and not comforted, I will build you with stones of turquoise, your foundations with sapphires. I will make your battlements of rubies, your gates of sparkling jewels, and all your walls of precious stones." God wants to be the strength we go to an art time of need and he will do as he promised. Even though our lives might be shaking up a little, he will comfort us and give us peace.

At times we began to idolize those people who we think are sane, but the longer we get to know these people we soon discover that they are not very same. Come on, no one is really completely sane, but we regret if we do not live up to the standards shown by today's media. So much of the media is not really a good idol. (**Exodus**) "You shall not make for yourself an idol in the form of anything in heaven above or on the earth beneath or in the waters below." To worship or idolize media personalities is wrong. Our only idle should be nothing less than Jesus Christ Our Lord. Why would you even want to idolize a person any ways? People always let you down, but Jesus Christ will always be by your side and comfort you. (**2Corinthians1:3–5**) Praise to the God and Father of our Lord Jesus Christ, the Father of compassion and the God of all comfort, who comforts us in all our troubles, so that we can comfort those in any trouble with the comfort we ourselves have received from God. For just as the sufferings of Christ flow over into our lives, so also through Christ our comfort overflows." This comfort is a free-gift, meaning that Jesus will be by our side through the mist of the storms.

Much of the time in our *pilgrimage toward recovery*, we tend to use God's name in vain! (**Exodus20:4**) "You shall not misuse the name of the LORD your God, for the LORD will not hold anyone guiltless who misuses his name." I must admit, for me this law is hard, because I am always having a slip of the tongue. If not for Jesus, I would go straight to hell on this a law alone. Although I know that through the redeeming blood of Jesus Christ all my sins our forgiven, even the ones of cursing. On this issue of the law, I am a work in progress, but one day the Lord will set me free from my wretched tongue. Sometimes life gets us so upset that we slip and curse God without meaning it. You should never let anyone get you this mad in your *pilgrimage toward recovery*. Anger only separates and causes friction with those we love the most. (**Hebrews4:3**) "Now we who have believed enter that rest, just as God has said, "So I declared on oath in my anger "they shall never enter my rest."" And yet his work has been finished since the creation of the world." Do not let your disability get you mad seek God for strength to use your weakness to show His strength. Let Creator of Heaven and Earth give you the rest you need.

In your *pilgrimage toward recovery*, you should always have some time set aside for just you and God. This is important to God and you, as you will soon discover. (**Exodus20:8-10**) "Remember the Sabbath day by keeping it holy. Six days you shall labor and do all your work, but the seventh day is a Sabbath to the LORD your God. On it you shall not do any work, neither you, nor your son or daughter, nor your manservant or maidservant, nor your animals, nor the alien within your gates." Sometimes this one becomes a difficult one to keep, because some types of work demand us to work on Sundays. A Sabbath Day does not always have to be on a Sunday, as long as you set aside one day out of the week that is to worship God. Make a day one, where you can praise the Lord to help him to show you how to prioritize your life for him and him alone. Also, this might be a good time to deal with the issues of why you are depressed. God wants to be part of your life even when you are depressed. For it is at that point, when he is carrying you in giving you rest!

For people like you and me, on the same *pilgrimage for recovery* to love and show respect to our parents is a very hard task, because many of us have been abused by our parents. (**Exodus20:12**) "Honor your father and your mother, so that you may live long in the land the LORD your

God is giving you." For me this law might have been the most difficult, because my father was an abusive alcoholic. How can an alcoholic father tell me not to drink, when he drinks himself? It just does not make sense, but he says to honor him. So I honor what is good and do not accept what is bad! I listened to my mom, because I respect her for sticking with him all these years and supporting me. Even though I respect my mother, my father is a different story! I love him pause he is my father and the Bible says I have to. I hate the way he treated me, but I love him for bringing me into this world and doing the best that he could in raising me. I do not blame him anymore, because it has given me a fire within me to succeed no matter how hard the circumstance might be.

Murder is murder, but they whitewash that crime. You may ask, what does murder have to do with depression? You will soon discover that it has a lot to do with depression. (**Exodus20:13**) "You shall not murder." Have you ever said, I wish he or she was dead or said I wish I were dead? If you answered yes, then you have committed murder in your heart. So when someone does wrong to you want what you say, because it can come back to bite you. (**Matthew5:21-22**) "You have heard that it was said to the people long ago, 'Do not murder, and anyone who murders will be subject to judgment." Jesus makes a crucial point in this verse by showing that what comes out of the heart is what we are thinking and therefore needs to be taking care of before a put into action. We should never say that we hate anyone no matter how much they hurt us, because hate can begin to grow inside us like a monster lurking to devour. You will be better off if you forgive and move on rather than the blow something way out of proportion.

When it comes to adultery many of us say I have never done this! These can be further from the truth and we realize, because it is really a matter of the heart. (**Exodus20:14**) "You should not commit adultery." Let us be a real with ourselves and realize we have all done this rather care to admit or not. Have you ever seen a girl in short shorts and tight shirt, thinking to yourself Wow? The way girls dressed in this day in age should be sin in itself, but we still have a choice rather to look away or stare. (**Matthew5:27-28**) "You have heard that it was said, 'Do not commit adultery; but I tell you that anyone who looks at a woman lustfully has already committed adultery with her in his heart." I now for myself

I have felt this when I've seen some young girl dressed provocatively making stare at her way she my mind that I was younger. Well if this is true and we have all committed adultery in our heart. The best way to stop doing this is to simply, look down so that your eyes do not see the provocatively dressed girl.

In dealing with depression, we all from time to time have cast faults judgments against a friend or foe. (**Exodus20:16**) "You should not give faults the witness against your neighbor." To say we have never done this we would be calling ourselves a liar for saying something so horrendous. We all get mad some times and say something that we really do not mean. To do so is human nature, but we still have to think before we say. Even if we say something that we did not think was bad, generally it was. (**Provebs14:25**) "A truthful man saves lives, but a false witness is deceitful." Deceitful is a strong word and when we are depressed such action hurt us, so why do it to someone else! Live as a purposeful person and do not give attention to anyone who would be the cause of spreading lies. You can be a better person than that.

At times when we are depressed, we go through moments when we wish that we had something that someone else had. It is hard to think any other way when you feel like you have no self-esteem. Sometimes there are those neighbors like to rub it in when they get something new that we do not have or plenty of work could not afford. (**Exodus20:17**) "You should not covet your neighbor's house." I know that for me this has been hard in the past; seeing a neighbor's wife in a bikini sunbathing in your mind begins to lust. Sometimes we wish we had a new car like our neighbors and regret them for having it. What you think heart in your heart is what generally comes out if you do not deal with it before it becomes something you regret. We must learn to be content in what we have or are we will never be happy. (**Philippians4:12–13**) "I know what it is to be in need, and I know what it is to have plenty. I have learned the secret of being content in any and every situation, whether well fed or hungry, whether living in plenty or in want. I can do everything through him who gives me strength." If we can do all things through Jesus Christ then why do we need anything else? The answer is nothing so just give it all to him. If it all things belong to God then we really have no reason to be angry or jealous.

Those that are Ten Commandments, we are to govern are lives and this is how one can live an extreme life. Jesus Christ is our Lord and nothing else will really matter, because with Jesus all things fall into place. When life gets stormy, because of what someone said or did to us let them like Jesus. Do this and you will grow in your *pilgrimage for the recovery* and you will discover peace and joy. It was said once before that it takes more muscles to frown than it does to smile, so why not just simply smiled. You will be glad you did! Shade off those times when we get depressed and grasp told of this concept. I know it is not easy, because I am still dealing with this one myself. I can say that I can make better person having discovered what it means, just simply smile.

If the Ten Commandments are the laws that we are to live by, then who are we! I think Dr. Neil Anderson summed this up in his book when he wrote about who we are in Christ: (**Romans 5:1**) "Since I am in Christ by the grace of God I have been justified completely forgiven and made righteous." (**Romans 6:1-6**) I died in Christ and died to the power of sin's rule over my life. (**1Corinthians 1:30**) I have been placed into Christ by God's doing. (**1Corinthians 2:12**) I have received the Spirit of God into my life that I might know the freely given to me by God. (**1Corinthians 2:16**) I have been given the mind of Christ. (**1Cortinthians 6:19-20**) I have been bought with a price. I am not my own; I belong to God. (**2Corinthians 1:21, Ephesians1:13, 14**) I have established, anointed and sealed by God in Christ, and I have been given the Holy Spirit as a pledge guaranteeing my inheritance to come. (**2Corinthians22:21**) Since I have died, I no longer live for myself, but for Christ. (**2Corinthians 2:14, 15**) I have been made righteousness. (**2Corinthians 5:21**) I have been crucified with Christ and it is no longer I who live, but Christ who lives in me. The life I live is in Christ. (**Galatians 2:20**) I have been blessed with every spiritual blessing. (**Ephesians 1:3**) I was chosen in Christ before the foundation of the world to be holy and I am without blame before him. (**Ephesians 1:4**) I am predestined determined by God to be adopted as God's son. (**Ephesians 1:5**) I have been redeemed forgiven and I am a recipient of His lavish grace. I have been made alive with Christ. (**Ephesians 2:5**) I have been raised up and seated with Christ in heaven. (**Ephesians 2:6**) I direct access to God through the spirit. (**Ephesians**

2:18) I may approach God with boldness freedom and confidence. (**Ephesians 3:12**) I have been rescued from the domain of Satan's rule and transferred to the Kingdom of Christ. (**Colossians 1:13**) I have been redeemed and forgiven of all my sins. The dept against me has been cancelled. (**Colossians 1:14**) I am firmly rooted in Christ and am now being built in him. (**Colossians** removed. (**Colossians 2:11**) I have been made complete in Christ. (**Colossians 2:10**) I have been buried, raised and made alive in Christ. (**Colossians 2:12, 13**) I died with Christ and have been raised up with Christ my life is now hidden with Christ in God. Christ is now my life. (**Colossians 3:1-4**) I have been given a spirit of power, love and self-discipline. (**2Timothy 1:7**) I have been saved and set apart according to God's doing. (**2Timothy 1:7, Titus 3:5**) I am sanctified and am one with the Sanctifier He is not ashamed to call me brother. (**Hebrews2:11**) I have the right to come boldly before the throne of God to find mercy and grace in time of need. (**Hebrews4:16**) I have been given exceedingly great and precious promises by God's divine nature. (**2Peter 1:4**) (Anderson, 1990-2000, pp. 57-59)

These few pages of confirmations and identity in Christ are very useful tools. Remember these and apply them as regulations to live by. If you know whom you are than this should make you better equipped to handle our Mental Illness. The Bible is the BASIC INSTRUCTIONS BEFORE LEAVING EARTH! Follow it and make it you manual for recovery and living life! The Bible should become your main source to use in discovering your-self. Our old ways are gone, so why live back there! We are one with Christ so live it! God had so much to teach you before you go and throw the keys away! Life has too much too offer if you only discover it. Every resource you will ever need is in the Bible, so learn it, breathe it, speak it and live it. God loves us to much to see us just give up and live as if we were dying! Let God and He will help you to see life again with new expectations and a hope for a better tomorrow. A life lived is a life set free from ones-self. Give up the humdrum way of living your life being recharged by the Holy Spirit and learn to succeed in areas of your life you never thought that you could. Almost to the end of the book, just two more chapters to go, hope use found some meaning in what you have read so far!

Dear Lord I have built my own prison dedicated by the dark walls and the shadows they cast. I am lost and cannot find my way home. Show me the rules for living and the regulation to live them. I fear that I lost my way! Give me peace from this tormented mind. Help me to understand the BASIC INSTRUCTIONS FOR LEAVING EARTH! Help me grow in your ways and recover from the broken spirit of mine. Make life real to me again dear Lord. Wake me up to the recharging power of your Holy Spirit. Teach me to become energized by your love.

Chapter XVI

The Key Words

The key words to our *pilgrimage toward recovery* are faith, hope and love. Each one is important, but they all need to be used with their undeniable effectiveness. To recover we must rediscover the meaning of these three common Word that in today's world is taken out of context. Each one is crucial and must be pulled apart and dissected to find the true meaning of each one in the reference they should be used. Why am I spending time on this? We have gotten this far in our *pilgrimage toward recovery* now it is time to talk about the words we seem to have lost in are times of disappear from past hurts. God is a caregiver and He wants to care for you, so let Him!

Faith in essence is the things hope for yet not seen; yet is still deeper than that. With faith comes discipline and beckons to us to endure hardship as children of God dedicated to His teaching and correction. For if God is not a loving father who disciplines his children than we cannot be called children of God. If we are not discipline than we are illegitimate children and not true children of God. We all have human fathers and if our parents truly loved us those parents would disciplined us, so how much more would the loving Father of our Spiritual man discipline us. Faith asked has children of God respectfully let God discipline us by his grace found in faith. Faith asked us to subject ourselves to loving God who created us! Faith is like a teacher who helps us understand and learn the loving nature of God. If God shows us mercy, He will not hold back His hand in from the discipline we reap for the consequences of our sins. Even though we go through hard times keep faith in God and through the Holy Spirit, he will teach us the wisdom we need to get through the sufferings.

Faith also is our strength in difficult times, because God uses this to shape us into the image he had designed us to be. Faith shows us nothing is impossible when we lean on God. (**John 14:12**) "I tell you the truth, anyone who has faith in me will do what I have been doing. He will do even greater things than these, because I am going to the Father." As believers in Christ we have strength send from God in heaven to keep us strong and succeed. In the Greek faith is: (pistis)—faithfulness, belief, and (pistos)—trust, worthy and believe—(pistoō)—to convince—continuance of (pistikos)—pure. In some context in the Greek faith is—(pisteuō)—to trust or entrust—(pistikos)—pure—(pisteuo)—to trust or entrust. Looking up faith in the Greek should broaden our perspective of faith giving us a deeper meaning of what is to have faith. Jesus Christ is reliable and trustworthy source and in him, we can become pure in heart. Jesus convinces us in the Word his love longing to be connected to us.

Hope is living knowing that we will receive the blessing of grace and love from our Creator. (**Job 13:15**) "Though he slay me, yet will I hope in him; I will surely defend my ways to his face." Despite the fact that Job did not know why he was suffering Job continued to trust God. Job not once in his suffering curse God, but stood steadfast ultimately in the end having God bless, Job. (**Psalm 62:5–6**) "He alone is my rock and my salvation; he is my fortress, I will not be shaken." King David although he stumbled many times, he knew he could find hope in Almighty God! That is where we should center our hope on for any chance of recovery. Hope in God is what makes live and live free. Discover this freeing concept of hope and you will discover that you have recovered and are on your way to recovering. (**1 Thessolonian 1:3)** "We continually remember before our God and Father your work produced by faith, your labor prompted by love, and your endurance inspired by hope in our Lord Jesus Christ." It is in the hope of Christ Jesus our Lord find a helping hand to reach out to in our *pilgrimage toward recovery*. I urge you to make Jesus Christ your reason to hope for change. Pray and Jesus is there to prep you for the steps you need to walk forward. Hope therefore, is are peace and rest in time of desperation.

Hope in Hebrew is (yahal) to wait for expectedly—(yahily)—to be in waiting—and (yahlel)—to wait for God and or for God to show himself, friendly. Why not take God's offer to be friendly too us? As we wait for God, he in turn waits for us to bring healing. As we begin to expect in God He likewise expects in us. It becomes an eternal union of hope that flows like and endless source of purifying water. In the Greek hope is (elpis)—expectations of—(elpizo)—put hope in or expect—(proelpizo) to be the first or be the forehand—(ekgamisko)—to give in to hope of marriage—(apelpizo)—to expect nothing in return. This makes quite an interesting thing to think about in light of the meaning of hope. What we expect come in our expectations of Christ first and he provides the final presence of hope. God knows our expectations before we ask, so our hope should be grounded in Holy marriage to the Priestly Groom (Jesus). The Lord is our hope and hope is a flame that ignites us in the mist of the overcast from the storms of this life. Hope gives us the ability to recover on a level of stability like, we never expected. Reach out to Jesus Christ for hope and everything you do will fall into place giving you rest and hope for a better tomorrow.

Love is an unconditional act of self-sacrifice toward another not looking for anything in return. Love looks at people's faults and accepts them without pre-judging them. Love accepts a person as a whole and does not hold faults against a person. Love sacrifices itself for another and is willing to give its life for another. Jesus Christ showed love by dying on the Cross rising from the dead so that we may share eternal life with him. True love is also patient in waiting for its counterpart to come around to the act of loving. God is more than patient; in his love for you (His Creation). To explain the true nature of love and what it means to you, must empty yourself of self and give all yourself for the work of others. Love is willing to give everything and loves until one can love more and even then never give up on loving.

In Hebrew love is (hesedz)—unfailing, devotions and or kindness. Love is also (hasad)—to conduct oneself as faithful in love in reference to a (hasadyah)—meaning God who is faithful—(hezeg)—our strength. If the love of God is unconditional and sacrificial and why cannot we devote ourselves to Him? We have a God who simply wants to love us, so just the hand of the Creator and He will let you fly on the ways of love. God is faithful in everything he does and He wants to take your and pain replacing it with his love. The act of love is a selfless act done for a complete stranger or a selfless act done for an enemy. Love shows no favorites, but is hopelessly devoted to the other. The act of love expects nothing in return, but a simple gesture of appreciation. God constantly throughout the Old Testament showed the Israelites unconditional love and devotion. He forgave them time & time again.

Love in the Greek referrers; (Philo)—to kiss—(Philemon)—beloved and love—(Philia)—friendship kind of love—(Philantho)—to mean and kindness and too be kind—also where get (Philos) and (Philia)—meaning friendship or to be friendly—(Synoomelio)—to converse with or two to talk in the act of love. God and throughout the Bible shows his love as He longs to give us a spiritual kiss. He wants to show us have loving-kindness, so in return we can love others with this same kind of love. His son Jesus showed the most selfless act which was dying on across! Jesus did this so that the Father and Son would be like a brother or friend. God is always there through His Son Jesus Christ. Nothing can break this bond of love and he searches for any & all opportunities to converse with his children (believers in Christ).

In all understanding of the truth about love, hope and faith, I know that God weeps too. We questioned God for everything we go through in life, but he has never left our side we just ran too far ahead. God bless them losers in the frail people of the world. We have hope in the fact that through our faith in Jesus Christ who conquered death so that we could know God's love. You may find a reason for giving amongst the challenges you face in life, but nothing can ever fill the void those challenges leave upon our soul. God is there with his hand out, such as reach out and take it. Do what it takes to take back control that has been stolen by your mental illness. What you think was a lifetime of part is closer than you think. Why think you must recover alone? God is there and a host of people in your same predicament so searched them out for the help you need.

Take joy in this one fact, that God loves us and at times seems over us with laughter and joyous words. Do not be blind and lost your feelings away and your self-indulgent prison of the fear. God has the keys and longs to set you free and dance a joyous dance of lavish joy. He longs to be our Father and give us an overall abundance of grace. For it is in His love that we find strength to journey on this *pilgrimage toward recovery*. Do not let your childhood abuse lead you on a course of self-destruction, but let the present hour of grief would be cleansed by the rain of God's tears. For as the rain and the snow come down from heaven, and do not return there until they have watered the earth, making it bring forth and sprout, giving seed to the sower and bread to the eater. So shall my word be that goes out from my mouth; it shall not return to me empty, but it shall accomplish that which I purpose, and succeed in the thing for which I sent it. For you shall go out in joy and be led back in peace; the mountains and the hills before you shall burst into song and all the trees of the field shall clap their hands. Instead of the thorn shall come up the cypress; instead of the brier shall come up the myrtle; and it shall be to the LORD for a memorial, for an everlasting sign that shall not be cut off. (**Isaiah, Chapter 55**)

Dear Lord, instruct me on the fine art of friendship to become a most precious friend, so I can befriend others. Help me to discover true friendship and love. Help me to have faith to move the mountains of depression that cultivate in my life. Give me the faith to pray with purpose! I feel need and I am in need of real faith. Teach me to have the faith of the men and woman of the Bible. Give me strength to love and be loved. Lavish your true love upon me! Educate me to keep hope for a better tomorrow. Lend a hand in my hope for recovery from mental illness. As I crawl through the dessert of my depression, help me to find my hope in you.

Chapter XVII

Success in Self-Discovery

Self-discovery comes when we not only find out who we are, but how we can come successful in recovery. What is success in recovery? In order to understand the answer we must have knowledge of success. The success I want to discuss is not like the world calls being successful, but what God considers successful! To God success is measured in what we do for others and not what we do for ourselves. God said of Jesus in many occasions when He showed selflessness, this is my Son whom I am well pleased! King David writer of most of the Psalms was successful in everything he did, because he relied upon God. Joseph one of Jacob's favorite sons was successful, because he stayed in the will of God. Job was successful, because even in the mist of extreme trials and testing he would not rebuke God. Paul who wrote most of the New Testament was successful, because he realized that God's grace was sufficient for him.

In the Hebrew, the word success is (salah2)—proper—to prevail, to grant properly and victorious. In the Aramaic, the word is (selah)—cause to prosper, to promote and to make progress. In the Greek—(nikē)—apparently a primary word; conquest (abstractly), that is, (figuratively) the means of success—victory. All these deviations or variables of the word success all have the same conclusion and that is success come from first promoting the success of others before our own success. Success is not the measure of a man, but the measure of a man is how many people he nudged to become successful. The world measure success with vain deceit or pride of the flesh, but God measures success by the heart of man. Society in a whole looks at the outside and judges based on false attempts to understand the heart of a person. If you truly want to recover than look beyond the stares of others and prove yourself to the world that you are better than that. "And have put on the new self, which is being renewed in knowledge in the image of its Creator."(**Colossians 3:10**) This renewal of knowledge equips you to live a life altered by God Himself. God will be with your every step of the way in your *pilgrimage toward recovery*. For it is a renewed mind full of purpose that grows and recovers. To find self-discovery go beyond what you know and set your sights on higher goals.

All success in life comes in God who gives us victory over depression and joy to our wounded heart. We will prevail if put our entire trust in Christ Jesus, because He will grant us a prosperous spirit and give us strength to find grasp self-discovery. Who is to blame for our inflictions? Is it our parents for bringing us up wrong? This may be hard to swallow for some, but it is our fault and our fault alone. We make the conscious choices that rule our lives or change our lives. Success will be made evident when we get off our "pity-pot" and go find a circle of friends to support us in this cruel world. We can never know true self-discovery unless we break down our self-made walls. Walls only keep people out and make us more depressed, so as a person in recovery we need to go beyond those walls and reach out to someone. The worst thing we can do for ourselves is go into hibernation mode blocking any chance of recovery. To hibernate is to lock ourselves away and that can be dangerous bringing us further and further from recovery. Self-discovery is finding the source in our own self-discover the power of Christ inside us.

What can we do to better ourselves? Simply, sup with Jesus Christ whom made the ultimate sacrifice. To do this means to stand against the faceless man inside all of us. "To forsake this meal and others means of grace such as prayer, fellowship, service and meditation to scripture—is to starve our hearts of Gods rich and necessary provision. We merit nothing, but profit considerably as we ourselves to the disciples of grace." (Smith, 2001, p. 208) Take the initiative and dine with the Lord at the "Masters Table" you will not be disappointed. There you will find water that flows like a waterfall that never runs dry. In my own personal self-discovery, it took me years to the important aspect and when I got there, I discovered what God already knew. That is the fact that self-discovery lies in going beyond your comfort zone and become a purposeful person secure and successful in their own *pilgrimage toward recovery*.

As a form of psychotherapy, writing of poetry or others writing varieties work as creative modes of discovering ones true potential; doing this you might learn how to visualize your problems and create ways to express them into applicable techniques to recovery. Most people with mental illness or disabilities, the creative process becomes an allusive therapy helping the person suffering to find his or her meaning of self-worth. During the 20th Century and into the 21th Century this form of creative therapy has been adapted in many psychiatric facilities. Such forms of therapy have importance on the development of the recovery process in the World! Implicating this therapy puts the focus on the struggling person ability to develop opportunities to become self-confident allowing them to interact with people in a positive and productive way.

Another thing that is seems to work is walk in nature enjoying God's beautiful creation. The stimulus that one receives activates the circuitry and neurotransmitters in the brain often resulting in feelings of extreme joy. It can be spelled out in the way people with many mental disorders might have unconsciously altered levels of dopamine sending mixed messages to the brain. Medicine can help fix the chemical problem, but it is up to us to deal with the emotional aspect of mental illness. I can relate to this fact, because without medication I am out of control and all over the place. This is where the "rubber meets the road" in fact, because when we are controlled and alert we begin to see where we really need help and that can be a scary place.

I know where you are at when feeling this way, because I feel the same way. When losing a job I began to worry and think I am nothing, but in all aspect to the truth that is an out and out lie; because God created me to be someone special to do His purpose for my life. Finding self-discovery in the broken world of Mental Illness is a hard task and I am learning this myself as I discover whom I am and where I am meant to be. The loss of my job recently the last two days has me feeling a bit overwhelmed, but thinking clearly, now maybe it is needed time to finish this book. I have to be reminded that whenever a door closes that God will open up another door better than the first. For me maybe not working is an open opportunity to write more and spend much needed time with the Lord. The Lord stand in wait for us to come to Him with all our cares, fears and doubts, so take the leap of faith. Go to the source of hope, Christ Jesus! No one knows suffering more than He does. He is the Suffering Servant of Isaiah 53!

Take the chance and learn to recover from your depression and anxiety. Once you ask Jesus into your heart asking Him to help you in your recovery you are on your way. Tap into the source and success will be in your grasp when you discover that self-discovery means self-discipline of old selfish-self. (**Proverbs 12:1**) "Whoever loves discipline loves knowledge, but he who hates correction is stupid." Here again we see the need to chasten instruction. Recovery is not a "free ride", it comes with a price and that is self-discipline. You might say I am so depressed I cannot think, but that is when discipline comes in handy. The Word of God teaches several times and is a standard in any recovery. Love avails, but love also brings the hurt to the surface. By doing, this love forces us to deal with the problem instead of pushing it down. The correct definition of success in recovery lies in a simple picture of a cube that to the struggling seems like and endless optical illusion. The cube is there and vivid, but through the eyes of someone who is depressed it becomes struggle or metaphor for a hurt with no way of defining successful recovery. The only thing that truly matters is that we are ready and comfortable with the achievement of self-discovery. It comes down to our taking responsibility for our success. Success in recovering from Mental Health related issues is a byproduct of our conscious choice not to be depressed.

Now you may be saying, everyone wants to recover from the anguish of depression, but it is so hard. That is the issue here we do not what to take the chance for fear of being hurt. To be in a constant state of recovery and self-awareness we have to discover that no one is the same, we are unique and deal with things differently. The conscious choice to recovery becomes clarity of purpose, persistent determination that accomplishes the purpose of recovery and self-discipline. The only catch is that the purpose for recovery is defined according to how we personally feel our definition of successful recovery is. Most pilgrims in recovery dig up old habits and borrowed definitions from the culture around us loosing focus. Clarity comes when you discover the courage to reflect and self-evaluate why you want to recover.

Your definition of successful recovery at times may be different from the next person, but different as it may it is where you need to find yourself! You need to take the initiative voluntarily, willingly and with courageousness to decide yourself to interject failure and loss, because in our greatest failures we find our greatest moments. We have to recreate our vocabulary that relates to the conversations we become part of in our daily lives. At this point in the book, I hope you have learned the negative talk and thinking only allows you to fall into a downward spiral of self-doubt. In times of failure, interject positive thinking and meditate on the Word of God. Find a scripture that touches you and think on it for a while and you might just feel a little better every time. Scientist have, said that when humans fear, they tend to paralyze and hide away. This is nothing new the Bible repeats this at least a dozen times in both the Old Testament and the New Testament. Let it be said that few of ever find ourselves managing fear in our lives. Self-discover is a defining mode of recovering from a life full of hardships, but must be taken seriously for us to ever discover, who we are and where we fit in.

Figure out ways of emerging from our fearful depression to become victorious in the battle for the mind. Face it there are times when we will feel a little unsettled and uneasy, but are masterpieces in the eyes of God and need to discover God's love. God is the author of our lives and we are the clay to molded and fastened into the image of His workmanship. When we call on God to be, successful that does not mean wealth or popularity, but successfulness in our emotional stability. Are actions toward each other should not be based upon rash decisions, but entirely under the will of God. (Proverbs 16:23) "A wise man's heart guides his mouth, and his lips promote instruction." Here again we see the need to chasten instruction. Recovery is not a "free ride", it comes with a price and that is self-discipline.

You might say I am so depressed I cannot think, but that is when discipline comes in handy. The Word of God teaches several times and is a standard in any recovery. Love avails, but love also brings the hurt to the surface. By doing, this love forces us to deal with the problem instead of pushing it down. Our own definition of success is similar to a picture that interprets who we are and become across our optical illusion that has been altered by years of neglect. Commit yourself to trouble spotting defining success in overcoming your depression in matters of comfortable and excited achieving success. True recovery refers to a choice to become successful by knowing what exactly recovery means to our goal of recovery. Recovery must become clear of purpose—relentless determination and willingness to accomplish a purpose of good health. A defining purpose in recovery comes by definition of successfully overcoming depression. Most of us become stuck, because we borrow wrong definitions from family, peers or our surrounding culture. In finding our self amongst the ruff, we need discipline that analyzes our emotions. Such discipline takes an act of will that goes beyond what we think as common.

Clarity in recovery requires the courage to reflect and self-evaluate our current path of recovery. The definition of success does not need to be different from others. It just needs to be what you voluntarily, willingly and courageously have decided for yourself in order to recover. Psychology tells us that as humans we experience fear it paralyzes us and it can make us run away not dealing with the source. Very few us every really try to manage our feelings instead letting fear get the best of us, not figuring that we can emerge victorious from the battle of depression and fear. "I eagerly expect and hope that I will in no way be ashamed, but will have sufficient courage so that now as always Christ will be exalted in my body, whether by life or by death." (**Philippians 1:2**) This, Christ that Paul says is exulted in us gives us strength to take courage in times of depression. Live life in victory instead of shame and you will find self-discovery.

The means of finding such self-discovery comes from our ability to let go of all the fears of the past and give it to God. We make the change in our life, not medicine, psychologist or any other means. Medicine only controls the chemicals that our out of order in our brain, it is up to recovery and us to grow. I am by no means against psychology or medication, but I do believe we are the only ones who find the courage needed to motivate ourselves to begin to recover. This was a challenge writing this book as it was for you reading it and using the tools in your own *pilgrimage toward recovery*. Much of we do is based on how we perceive the world around us, so finding self-discovery are view has to be clear. If a mirror is smudged how we see ourselves clearly, the image becomes blurry. In the same aspect if are view of the world is not clear then we will not see a clear image of ourselves in it.

My final words of advice in finding self-discovery lies in the fact that we our own image of self-discovery. Things may change around us and may cause us from time to time to be depressed, but we make the choice of how we deal with it when we do. Life does not have to be difficult and full of depression and anxiety, because God holds the cards and He will never deal us a losing card. Life is planned by the Creator! "When times are good, be happy; but when times are bad, consider: God has made the one as well as the other. Therefore, a man cannot discover anything about his future." (**Ecclesiastes 7:14**) God knows us and knows our future even before it comes into existence, so there is nothing that He will do that we cannot handle. He is the God who created you so He knows and will guide you to finding your true self. "And I trust that you will discover that we have not failed the test." (**2Chronicals 13:16**)

Dear Lord I am trying to find my own self-discovery and finding it hard to do so. Help me Lord to redefine who I am in light of your love, so I can become a better pilgrim in recovery. I pray for strength where there is none and for peace where is needed. My whole life has become on a course to exist in you. I know that you will never let me down, but be with me every step of the way in this *pilgrimage toward recovery* I have chosen. Take this wounded shell of a person and make me into the image you want it to be!

Amen

Bibliography

Anderson, D. N. (1990-2000). *Victory Over the Darkness.* Ventura, CA, USA: Regal Books.

Dr. M. Scott Peck. (1987). *The Different Drum.* New York, NY, USA: Touchstone Publishing.

Lewis, P. P. (2010, June 6). Road Trip. Pinellas Park, FL, USA: Park Place Weseyan Church.

Luccado, M. (2005). *Cure For The Common Life.* Nashville, TN, USA: Thomas Nelson.

Meyers, R. (n.d.). esword NIV. *www.esword.net.* Franklin, TN, USA: Rick Meyers.

NIV. (1999). *Rick Meyers.* Franklin, TN, USA: Rick Meyers.

Nouwen, H. (1999). *In the Name of Jesus.* New York, NY, USA: The Cross Publiishing Company.

Osteen, J. (2004). *Your Best Life Know.* New York, NY, USA: (Faith Works) Hachette Book Group.

Peck, D. M. (1993). *Denial of the Soul.* New York, NY, USA: Random House.

Peck, D. M. (1987). *Different Drum.* New York, NY, USA: Touchtone Publishing.

Peck, D. M. (1979). *The Road Less Traveled.* New York, NY, USA: Touchstone Publishing.

Peck, D. M. (1997). The Road Less Traveled and Beyond. In D. M. Peck, *The Road Less Traveled and Beyond* (p. 109). New York, NY, USA: Touchstone Publishing.

Smith, P. S. (2001). *Obects of His Affection*. West Monroe, LA, USA: Howarrd Publishing.

Warren, P. R. (2002). *The Purpose Driven Life*. Grand Rapids, MI, USA: Zondervan Publishing.

Warren, R. (2002). *The Purpose Driven Life*. Grand Rapids, MI, USA: Zondervan Publishing.